Nine Journeys

*Stories of Women
Who Found Their Own Paths to Success*

Paula Fortini, Kathy Eber, Michelle Prima, Kari Skloot, Ashlee Niethammer,
Dorothy Deemer, Pam Labellarte, Linda Polhemus, Bonnie Richtman

outskirtspress
DENVER, COLORADO

Outskirts Press, Inc.
http://www.outskirtspress.com

ISBN: 978-1-4787-5909-6

Outskirts Press and the "OP" logo are trademarks belonging to Outskirts Press, Inc.

PRINTED IN THE UNITED STATES OF AMERICA

*This book is dedicated to every would-be entrepreneur
who dares to go down her own path.*

Contents

Foreword

Something happens to your worldview when you become self-employed. You set your course and work without a net. There are no scapegoats. You live in the moment with your accountability. Flying under the radar is not a strategy for success. Breaking the sound barrier is.

Entrepreneurs have a strong common bond. We've traded our airplanes for hang gliders. There are no runways or control towers. We choose our departure times and locations trusting our instincts to perform a safe landing at the end of a very wild ride.

So why did nine self-propelled women commit to write this book? It's not like we have lots of spare time. We did it to encourage other women who might be holding back because of fear or lack of confidence. You're not alone. Every one of us wanted a more satisfying career, and each of us fought back fear and doubt to take a chance.

Goaded by a comment that most books on entrepreneurship are written by men, Paula Fortini became the lightning rod that convinced a group of women business owners to join her in writing and publishing the personal stories that led to our own entrepreneurial ventures.

Even as we publish, another friend tells us she has opened her own salon after working years in another one. In her words, "I knew I was in trouble when my willingness to lose it all became stronger than my willingness to stay and work for something I didn't believe in."

Entrepreneurial women are not new to the planet. Today about 1 in 10 working women are self-employed. According to Fast Company, "Women with established businesses ranked their happiness nearly three times as high as women who are not entrepreneurs or established business owners."

The authors of this book are thrilled to share our stories about finding our paths without looking back. It wasn't easy. But then we weren't looking for easy. We were looking for purpose.

Why us? Why not us? Why not you?

Foreword and cover copy by Kathy Eber.

It Started With a Dare

By Paula Fortini, Educational Program Developer, Speaker

YES, MY CAREER changed on a dare! Who does that? I guess I do! It all began with what I thought was planning for my retirement, at age 35. I decided I needed a new degree that would enable me to work well into my retirement doing something I would be physically able to do, and something I would enjoy later in life. I was thrilled with myself for looking so far ahead and not only planning for my financial future, but doing something that would help others.

I decided I wanted to get a new degree in Non-Profit Management. Classes were offered in the evening and I could complete it in just over a year. I encouraged a friend to complete the new degree with me. So she and I began our new venture. Let me just say, schooling at middle age is not as much fun as it was at 21 on a large Big Ten campus. But with a full time job and a young child at home, it was nice to know I would have weekly time with a dear friend and get an education all at the same time. So off we went to be college students (again) at 35.

Throughout all the classes my friend heard story after story of how un-happy I was working with my current employer (to remain nameless to protect the identities of those still employed there). After our final class, the instructor was very excited about my final project establish-ing a nonprofit where we would teach families that were learning

English as a second language. Our focus would be the youngest children so they could start kindergarten on an equal playing field. The parents would be our team to help their child achieve; and in the process, they would become more confident in their English use.

My gracious friend who had listened to me complain week after week basically said, "Put up or shut up. This is your chance. Turn this project into a for-profit and quit your job, or stop complaining!" Nothing like a friend to lay it on the line. Thanks KS. You planted the seed! I am happy to say she has also recently started her own business writing grants for nonprofits. That one phone call to her saying "let's start planning for retirement" changed both of our lives!

Not one to ever turn down a dare, I decided my friend was right. I couldn't complain to everyone and do nothing to correct my unhappiness. So a few months later, after 15 years of teaching, I quit my job. I left behind a pension, tenure, and the solid belief in my previous career. Teachers don't go into teaching for anything but the love of what they do. I was now walking away from that love. I had nightmares, as did another friend who dreamt that I would end up losing my house and living in a panel van if the business didn't make it. Thanks JG. I won't name you either! At the time your dream terrified me, but now I can laugh. In June of 2003, exactly one week after I left my teaching career, Lil Scholars was born.

For any business owner naming your business is a tricky proposition. I brainstormed with anyone and everyone who would listen. In the beginning I was unsure the market existed for what I was opening - a foreign language program for young children ages 3-6. To be safe I named the business Lil Scholars with the logic that if language didn't work out, I could make scholars out of many different areas and keep all my branding and name. I registered the name and opened a bank account. In my first week of business I signed up two clients. Twelve years later both are still with me. Thanks for believing in me Cherished Children Early Learning Center and Old School Montessori. Lil Scholars was on its way to being profitable!

Many sleepless nights followed. A fear of the unknown and the lack of a consistent pay was worrisome, but a loving husband and his belief in what I was doing kept me on track. From that very first year until now, 12 years later, I increased my revenue every year (except the 2008 recession).

I will never wonder what would have been. I KNOW what would have been. I am living it! As a typical type A person, I am in control and make my own destiny; I wouldn't have it any other way. However, before I continue, let me just say owning my own business is HARD work and the hours are LONG. But my schedule was flexible and enabled me to spend precious time with my preschool son. I was able to grow the business as he grew, and play with him more than many of my peers who had children the same age. I wouldn't trade that time for anything. Please don't think I am a believer that everyone can be an entrepreneur, because I don't. It is hard work even for those of us that want to. But for the right person it can be a truly life altering decision.

Then there were two

After a few years the business grew to more than I could manage myself; a problem I never anticipated, but I was thrilled. I needed to clone myself. Alas, with science not able to do that for me, I had to hire others. Again this was a scary proposition. Not only was I responsible for myself and my bills, but I was contemplating being responsible for someone else and their bills.

Finding the first members of my team took time and a lot of interviewing. It was vital to hire people who shared my vision and would help me learn to be an employer. At this point I knew I needed to learn myself. Being a good teacher is not the same as being a good employer. I didn't have all the answers and needed teachers who could teach me to be a good boss. A great leader knows how to utilize the team and lead, but is open to suggestions and delegates. You must have a strong belief in your team to delegate and trust.

It is now 12 years later and my first teacher is still with me. She has since had a baby and taken a full time teaching job; but she still works for me part time. I value her most for teaching me how to be a leader. Thanks GO! Hey look at that. Her initials mean go. I guess it was meant to be that she taught me to GO.

Lil Scholars grows up.

Growth is difficult but a necessary step in any business. Take it with care. I wish I knew then what I know now, and had hired a business coach to move to the next step. A business coach would have been a nice team member. Lucky for me I learned that in a few years!

The biggest change was when the business outgrew the business model. Suddenly clients were calling asking if we taught older kids. My original mission was very clear: I believed we best served children ages 3-6. However, as my mastermind partners know, I am always willing to change to meet the clients' needs. So I decided to adapt our program to meet the needs of older students.

Lil Scholars began our elementary program at the request of parents who liked our approach and services. If you listen hard enough, your clients will tell you exactly what they want/need. FLASHBACK: Listening to clients is vital for any business owner. One day while I was singing with a group of children, a 3 year old boy said to me, "Miss Paula, why don't you put our songs on a CD so I can listen to them in the car and sing with my mom?" Out of the mouths of babes! How did I never think of that before? While your business is growing up, I highly suggest you listen attentively to EVERYONE - even the three year olds. Take action on only the advice that works for you, but always listen. You never know where or when great advice will come. I am just lucky my little guy didn't ask for royalties!

Westward Ho (East, North and South, too)

Now that I had a solid curriculum and a new song CD, thanks to my young 3 year old student, it was time to grow again. Though I had nearly exhausted my marketplace, I knew there were more children outside of our market area. The idea of packaging our curriculum, parent materials and the infamous song CD came to mind. I changed the name to Lil Language Scholars to better explain what we do, and trademarked it so I could sell our curriculum nationwide.

All I needed was a phone to contact schools outside the area and sell what I know works. Wow, now I am a salesperson. Blink your eyes and your role changes. At least this time it wasn't on a dare. I am still selling my curriculum nationwide as a nice little turn-key "Language in a Box" program for schools.

Did we make the grade?

As I see it, I made the grade. I had a little idea that was nothing more than a project I had to do to finish a class. By the way, I got an A on the project. So taking the project and turning it into a business was simple. Take an A and make it a Type A business. It does help that I am truly a Type A personality as well!

So here I sit continuing to grow this business with the advice of every person willing to talk to me. I listen and listen some more. I don't take all the advice, but I do take much of it. Parents love our programs, kids love our programs, and our teachers love what they do. Could it get any better than that? I doubt it. I just need to keep growing at a pace that makes me comfortable.

My brother, a self-employed businessman with multiple businesses himself often says, "You could make so much more money if you worked harder." Well, you know what? He's right. However, I work to live, not live to work. This is advice I have chosen not to take. I love you Steve, but in this way we are different! I enjoy what I do; but let's face it…it is work. I want free time! I want hobby time! I want family time! I don't want it all—I want a nice balance, and that I have. So in my scheme of life, I have earned myself an A.

Public schools come a callin'. What's a girl to do?

Ten years into my business, I received a call out of the blue from a public school. A principal from a local school district said, "We need a teacher starting next week at the beginning of the school year. Someone suggested I call you. Would you like to schedule an interview?"

The original fear returned with a vengeance. Had I been smart to give up my tenure and guaranteed pension? Maybe this was my way back in. Retirement is after all something to be planned for.

Being in business for ten years had given me some courage so I re-plied back, "What could you pay me? I know my worth. I don't want to waste your time with an interview if you can't pay me what I am worth." She gave me the figure and I wrote it down. I took the infor-mation and promptly called my accountant, two dear friends, my husband, and of course, my parents. Absolutely no one suggested returning to the schools was a good idea. My accountant reminded me of my successes and said, "You would be crazy to give up what you built. This is a step in the wrong direction." So after a polite call back to the school, my story continues with Lil Language Scholars. Thanks GB. You are right. That would have been a bad decision for me!

Time for dare number two. Who makes career decisions on dares? Who does that? Oh that's right, I DO!

Lil Language Scholars now pretty much runs itself. I have contemplated franchising many times. I have all the paperwork done and the process is ready thanks to my business coach. I still would be willing to sell a franchise but I have yet to find the PERFECT person! The program is set up and ready, but the right people have not yet come forward. Call me if you are that person!

For the second summer in a row I got a call from a charter school. This time I politely suggested that I might be able to help them find a teacher, but that I was not interested. Much less drama this time, and a self-assured decision that they cannot offer me what I have built for myself. I will refrain at this point from explaining my thoughts on the current demands upon teachers and the state of education in America. That's a whole other book.

Shortly thereafter I was explaining the unsolicited calls from the public schools to a friend, and that I often contemplated reentering the school system since Lil Language Scholars pretty much runs itself. He said, "Maybe you need to build your business into more than Lil Language Scholars. What else excites you? If Lil Scholars was only part of a bigger business what else could/would you do?" Enter DR and his dare to make my business bigger.

I sat down and took a hard look at what I could do that would complement Lil Language Scholars. One of the things I had missed the most is the opportunity to speak at large conventions. Over the years of teaching I had presented at conferences and loved it. I often have said, give me a topic and a group of people and I will speak. So the idea of speaking, coaching, and the burning desire to help senior citizens enjoy their retirement more, yielded my new business venture.

I tossed a lot of names around and settled on Family Scholars. Family Scholars enabled me to maintain my brand but grow into three sub-categories: SR Scholars, Lil Language Scholars and Self Scholars. Ultimately I would like to add Canine Scholars (they are family too) and offer dog training. But I guess I have to wait for another dare for that!

Birth of Family Scholars

"Congratulations!" my business associates said. I felt like a new mom again, a little uncertain, a little nervous, a little concerned that I might not do it right. But the dare was on the table so it was time to begin. As I write this book, Family Scholars is only two months old; but I have already scheduled speaking engagements for SR Scholars, re-branded my websites and designed the templates for all of our educational materials.

As I proofread of my section of this book in a local coffee shop, a teacher I am interviewing for Lil Language Scholars asks what I'm working on. So I explain. A woman sitting near us comes over and asks about the book. She then invites me to a women's group that meets monthly and asks if I am willing to become a notable professional for them. Who says no to that? So I add a meeting with a new group of women to my schedule two days from now. That's how it works. Let me say, this ride is a bit bumpy (just like the first time), but I am in for the long haul (just like I was on the first dare).

What I have learned

- Always have fear; it makes you work harder. Never give in to the fear or you will give up. Don't show your fear. People like a self-confident, yet not arrogant, business owner.

- Don't look back. I made a decision NOT to do this. Every decision has good and bad. It never did anyone any good to look back with regret. Even when times are tough believe you did what you did for a reason, good or bad. You are a bigger, better person now than you were then. And as I always tell my students "you learn more from your mistakes than you do from your successes." Nothing is perfect so keep moving forward. Who knows if the past would have been what you remembered? So why question it!

Why would I do it all over again, even with the bumps and bruises?

Being self-employed is hard work. Yes, there are perks but it is ALWAYS hard work. You are never off the clock. At this moment in time it is late August on a Sunday evening and I am working, albeit working while sitting outside on my deck. At the same time I am talking to my mom on the phone. (Don't tell her I am typing while I am listening, although she can probably tell. Sorry, Mom.) With that said though, YES, a little bit louder now. YES. I would do it all over again. Even during a recession when times are tough, there is nothing like knowing you are responsible for your own success (and failure). As a dear friend LS always says, "There is enough work for everyone. If you want more work, go get it."

So in the true nature of Family Scholars and Paula Fortini…I DARE YOU to go do whatever you want to do. Set your mind to it and enjoy the ride! Remember the bumps make it more fun…just like on a school bus!

Special Thanks

THANKS to those I mentioned above for guiding me to live the life I love, and to:

My family - for the many years of support and care when I needed it most

KS-I owe it all to you!

JG-for making me laugh when I was so scared

GO-for trusting in me as my first teacher

DR-for the second dare that forced me to be bigger and better

LS-for your inspiration and for allowing me to learn from you; you have and will reach so many more through me!

AND to the many other family and friends who were always there when I had questions. You know I ask anyone with more knowledge than I have when I need it. That's the danger in calling me a friend. ☺ I try to respect your time and knowledge, but I probably ask more than I should. Please know you are much appreciated!

Enjoy life,

Paula

About the Author

Paula Fortini, MS Ed is the owner/founder of Family Scholars. Family Scholars educates the whole family: The littles, with Lil Language Scholars, a Spanish Language program for ages 3-12; the seniors, with a SR Scholars program that helps senior citizens and their caregivers have an enjoyable retirement both mentally and physically; and finally those who need a bit of guidance to make the best of where they are (both in business and in life), SELF Scholars, a program aimed at public speaking and coaching. Like the message delivered by flight attendants, *"For those traveling with someone who might need help, put your oxygen mask on first; then assist others,"* the Self Scholars message is "Help yourself first so you can be better for others!"

Paula is available for speaking engagements to inspire others to reach their best. Contact her at: info@lilscholars.com or author@family-scholars.com to discuss topics and dates available.

Family Scholars is proud to have helped myriads of people to become the best they can be. Please join us on our quest of educating. After all you are now part of Family Scholars. For speaking engagements, coaching, or curriculum contact info@lilscholars.com

Inexplicably Hopeful:
Lessons Learned Along the Way

By Kathy Eber, Freelance Writer

"If you decide that God has called you to the profession of novel writing, you are insane." – Jack Woodford, 1948

"If you're called to the profession of freelance writing - what can I say? - a sense of humor is not optional." – Kathy Eber, 2014

I have a friend who, when asked as a toddler what he wanted to be when he grew up, said, "a pilot, of course." And that's exactly what he became. That kind of long range clarity has always eluded me. Because lots of things interested me, the only thing I was sure of was that my mind would change as often as my clothes. So I ran, slid, stumbled, climbed and fell through the twists and turns of life looking for my path to the center of the universe.

Now in hindsight it's easy to see where the lessons were learned, and how they led to my selling my writing skills all over town as a freelancer.

1 The early nerd loves the word.

I've always enjoyed words – how they sounded, how they went to-gether, and what pictures they painted. That little kid walking around the house repeating the same word over and over again was me. I loved reading and critiquing billboards on family vacations. And find-ing a string of Burma Shave ads was the supreme highlight of any trip. "Don't pass cars – on curve or hill – if the cops don't get you – morti-cians will – Burma Shave! Can you find some more of those, Dad?"

By 6th grade, writing sentences for each of the week's ten new spelling words was so mind-numbingly boring that I got permission to use all the spelling words in a story instead. Each Friday the Dr. Destructo serial storyline changed based on the words chosen by the teacher. Didn't think I could do it, did you Mrs. Homer?

Lesson 1: Write for yourself. It can be very entertaining.

I always liked researching and writing essays and papers. Buried in notes from dull encyclopedia volumes for a paper on Stonewall Jackson, I couldn't wait to retell the story in my own words. There was always a way to make it more fun and accessible for others like me who hated slogging through text books.

Lesson 2: The best storytelling starts with the audience in mind.

Then there's the desk thing. As kids we played for hours pretending we were business owners. The best part was the desk. I liked having my own big desk with a phone, a calendar and a stack of very impor-tant looking papers. Somewhere in my subconscious I posted a note that said 'must have cool desk.'

Lesson 3: Every one needs a desk.

In 8th grade I won First Place and $2 in an essay contest for writing about what it was like to sleep with brush rollers in my hair. If you don't know what I'm talking about, forget it. You don't want to know. Stick with bed head.

Lesson 4: Writing can bring fame and fortune.

English class was fun, but turned me into my own worst critic and an obsessive compulsive speller. (I still misspell words, and the shame is awful.) When I hear a word, I have to visualize it. And when I see a word I don't know, I have to know how to pronounce it and how to use it. I even call businesses whose names I can't pronounce just to hear them answer the phone. ("Hello, Roehl Trucking.")

I give most of the credit for being a word wrangler to my mom whose verbal and written skills were impeccable; she wasn't shy about correcting me day or night either. There *weren't no* tolerance in our household for double negatives and the wrong tense. She is the only person I knew who ended her letters with 'more anon' instead of 'later.' A voracious reader, she no doubt worried I was spending too much time climbing trees, and not enough time reading. I bored easily and didn't really understand the page turner until Nancy Drew showed up.

Though I loved the pen at an early age, it wasn't until college that I started to appreciate the real power of writing. Before entering freshman year I wrote an impromptu essay so the school could assess my writing skills. From a list of subjects, I chose 'A country's advertising reflects its culture.' Boom! I didn't have to take Freshman Comp and got four credit hours of A.

Lesson 5: This writing stuff IS mightier than the sword.

College Freshman Reading changed me forever. We all read 10 assigned books on a particular theme and discussed them. Our theme was Revolution. (Hey, it was the sixties.) Anatomy of a Revolution, Portrait of a Decade, Black Rage, civil disobedience, Martin Luther King, Henry David Thoreau, Thomas Paine…

Writing from a platform for social change was a breath of fresh air for me. I devoured those books, and looked forward to class discussions. That year I dumped fiction until The Thorn Birds.

The clever word play of advertising was great fun and the most stimulating of all my business classes. We made up tag lines and print ads for both real and imaginary companies. I worshipped Mary Wells Lawrence, the only female household name on Madison Avenue, and learned the names of all the big agencies in Chicago. Would I fit there? People who know me can stop laughing now.

I really didn't see myself on Madison or Michigan Avenue. I couldn't bring myself to honestly convince people they had to have something or risk being shunned by society. Instead I saw myself working for the Ad Council doing public service ads. I knew I needed to write what I believed in. It was a moot point anyway. I took a break from college and got married.

Lesson 6: Without authenticity, writing is meaningless.

2 School's over. Get to work.

The entry level jobs that followed made me homesick for writing challenges. So I volunteered to write a company newsletter at the store where I sold pianos. When my kids were little I scribbled song lyrics in a spiral notebook, and penned letters to the newspaper for the thrill of being published.

The idea of working for a broadsheet was a romantic fantasy, but there were no summer jobs on the dailies for teen writers. Years later, with kids in school, the opportunity arose to sell ads for a small independent newspaper. That relit the flame. At first I was a little nervous about how minimalist the place was. The office was one room of a house turned commercial rental. Then I met the staff and I knew. I was in the right place.

I learned the organization, the paper distribution routes, and how to sell advertising. I was offered the chance to write about literally anything. But the expectations that came with a byline terrified me. I felt I was on the precipice of something.

Eventually I fought back performance anxiety and wrote my first story about a snowy owl that had blown off course and landed on the roof of the federal building. After writing and rewriting it on an old Remington at the kitchen table, I winced when the publisher read out loud, "*Probably no one felt the owl's presence more keenly than the local pigeons. C'mon, Kath, probably?*" Then he put a big red line through 'probably' and added 'certainly.'

I was mortified. My fragile ego was bruised. How could I be a feature writer after that? Nevertheless, the paper went to press, and I hid underground. Then I saw the story in print. I was published! I read it again. It sounded way better in newsprint. Oh yeah, and no one laughed (or read it).

Lesson 7: Despite your effort, sometimes no one cares.

Now I didn't worry so much about whether someone liked what I wrote, but whether they read it at all. With incredible patience and mentoring from the publishers, I learned to appreciate constructive criticism and got more confident behind the typewriter. I became aware of the community around me and the stories that were unfolding every day. New businesses opened and brought opportunities for me to share their stories with our readers. I was in awe of their courage.

Selling advertising wasn't easy, but it paid the bills. Every bump in the road taught me something. One advertiser lived to bring ad reps to tears. Others used me as entertainment, and then sent me away. Dealing with different kinds of business owners was a real eye opener (looks like a can opener, but made for eyes).

At one low point I drove to an appointment with a restaurant owner to sell an ad. It was winter and nearly dark when I set out for Bay City. The gauge on my old gas guzzler was hovering in the lower eighth of a tank. When I got there, the waitress sat me in a booth and asked if I wanted coffee. So I sat and sat.

After forty minutes it was clear the owner was not going to show up. I looked at the coffee cup I emptied three times and realized I couldn't pay for it. With no credit card or a dime on me, I was embarrassed. I was also too new to realize that the waitress understood the situation and fully expected it to be complimentary. I put on my coat and saw that my glove had fallen under the table. As I bent down to reach it, I found some change on the floor. Cue the harp music. Proudly I left it on the table for the waitress. I swore I would never forget it as long as I lived.

I drove back home that night with no sale, no gas and no reason to be hopeful. The next day the crew was back typesetting stories, laying out pages, setting up interviews, scheduling photo shoots and making lists of ad prospects. The world didn't end. Good and bad, life went on. At the end of the week we all celebrated the good. On Monday we continued our fight against the bad.

Local businesses didn't always buy ads from me, but they became my friends, my peers, my role models and a big part of the new world I was creating for myself. They shared their frustrations and challenges, and together we all found ways to survive. These times gave me strength and a growing sense of who I really was.

Lesson 8: Pay your dues. You'll get them back with interest.

The freedom at the publication was intoxicating. I collaborated with wonderful people and got to work for a brave entrepreneur. Despite the ongoing financial struggle to go to press, thirty-five years later the publisher is a local icon. He could have joined the family law practice. But nothing could keep him from his destiny.

Lesson 9: A true calling can trump Maslow's basic needs.

Had I stayed at my first boring bank job rather than jumping into the deep end, I would have been making a healthier living by now instead of using paper towels and a strainer to make coffee. Then again, had I missed those five wonderful and inspiring years of creative license and economic struggle, I doubt I would be working for myself right now.

During those years I met, interviewed and wrote about business owners, local leaders and celebrities. I wrote reviews. I learned a ton about the media, local politics and the importance of telling the story. It was more empowering than anything I had ever done before.

The struggle only made the reward sweeter. During those lean years the work itself fed my soul. My Spartan lifestyle actually fueled the starving artist in me. Spiritually I wanted for nothing. Those times were some of the toughest and best of my life.

Eventually practicality demanded that I leave the paper for more gainful employment. The recession of the early 80's hit everyone hard, especially those businesses that could no longer afford to advertise. As much as I hated to admit it, the financial struggle began to outweigh the joy. So I traded the fourth estate for the seventh circle of hell, home for sell outs. It was a very sad day for me, and the beginning of a new phase I call IOTYWA - It's only temporary. You'll write again.

Lesson 10: Creative fulfillment is a luxury you can't always afford.

3 Tales from IOTYWA and the corporarium

Corporarium, n. [corporate terrarium] a steamy high-powered work environment where you can artistically a) bloom or b) sweat to death.

During IOTYWA I began chasing money instead of journalistic relevance. You can't eat relevance. You have to be practical sometimes. So I took a job in car sales. Selling cars was claustrophobic after the freedom of the newspaper. But with encouragement from the manager, I hung in there. When I was done hanging a year later, he offered me a management position and a place on the advertising committee. I liaised with the ad agency, wrote copy and became a radio voice for the service department. Now that was fun!

The dealership was a one-of-a-kind adventure that inspired (and may still spawn) a screenplay. But I was ready for something more than I could find in Saginaw at the time.

Infused with hopes and dreams, I moved back to Chicago and became an outside sales rep for a company selling microfilm equipment, ironically something I used in my first office job as a teenager.

It gave me a hard core education about the city and suburbs, and expanded my world exponentially. From there I became a loan officer. I finally finished college through independent study, and eventually went on to sell microfilm services. I liked life in the big pond.

Selling cars, equipment, mortgages and services taught me a lot about self-discipline, persistence, prospecting, fear and rejection. Outside sales was a good path to independence for me, because as a rep I essentially ran my territory like a business. For the most part I had to choose my targets and go after them by myself. I was my dad's daughter – fearless and determined - but only half the salesman my brother is. So sales and competitive rankings motivated me for a while. And then they didn't.

Though I left the world of commission sales, I learned the joy of the sale thanks to some excellent leaders. I would draw on that when I began working with my own clients.

Lesson 11: Be grateful for tough love from the universe.

Though I was making a decent living, my need for creative expression was unfulfilled. Hitting sales numbers was not enough purpose for me.

I was fantasizing about joining the Peace Corps when a headhunter called about interviewing for a sales development position with a global manufacturer. Hmm…salary instead of commission, paid vacation, and no more living out of my dumpster on wheels (what we sales reps called our vehicles when they filled up with papers and drive-thru refuse). A big job in corporate America was definitely a doorway to new hope.

So I found a good resume writer who worked out of her home. That was the first time I consciously thought about what it would be like to work for myself as a writer. I never forgot it.

Lesson 12: Let other writers inspire you.

I got the job and loved it. I got a reliable car. I got my pilot's license. Instead of lonely cold calls, I was collaborating with resellers, product engineers and marketers. Communications was such an integral part of my new job that I got my Mojo back. I buddied up with marketing communications (MARCOM) and got to write my own copy for mailings, collateral, and press releases. I volunteered to help with video shooting and editing, and eventually became the go-to script writer.

My job morphed into a marketing position which opened up more experiences like advertising, videos and trade shows. I spent my days doing three of my favorite things – writing, marketing and learning. I learned about product management and branding. As part of a team I helped bring new technology to market around the world. The message became the thing, and I got to write it.

Lesson 13: Companies need good writing to grease the wheels of commerce.

I suppose I would have stayed longer than six years if not for the ceiling I was hitting or my need for change. Okay, my ego would not be denied. I wanted more of a say in the strategic marketing of the company, but was hamstrung in my current position. So I pursued a higher managerial role in MARCOM at another global manufacturer. I couldn't wait to try out my leadership skills at the new venue, as a boss.

Lesson 14: Ego, old friend, be careful what you wish for.

Being the head of a department was new for me. I had a talented, creative and energetic team. Our brainstorming sessions were the envy of everyone else, because we were drawing on the walls instead of pounding erasers. Life was good.

Thanks to some great recommendations, we worked with wonderful freelance vendors for graphic design, photography, video and even copywriting. I was most at home when doing project work with these kindred spirits.

Lesson 15: Let other entrepreneurs inspire you.

Global responsibility added dotted lines from six more countries, each with their own agenda. What an education. I successfully learned the complexities of sustaining a consistent message within the context of multiple cultures. It was pretty cool seeing my words printed in different languages around the world.

Unfortunately, I was frustrated with the hours I spent managing up and across the organization. Work became an endless barrage of meetings, conference calls, reports, and power struggles. The more time I spent managing, the less time I spent doing what I do best. Creative starvation was choking the life out of me.

Except for some stellar mentors (eternal thanks), I let the all-consuming agenda of the company and fears of unemployment subvert my dreams and happiness. I'd just put out the uncomfortable fires and worry about myself later. But later never came. I lost touch with who I was and what I wanted. Like the months following a bad breakup, when asked what I liked to do, all I could say was, "I don't remember."

By now the joy of management was all but gone. I dreamed of being in a place where I could abandon politics and communicate openly.

Taking a lower position would only give me less of a voice. Something was churning in my gut. The three hour commute on top of eleven hour days generated 'endless sound and fury, signifying nothing'[2] that made me happy.

[2] Macbeth, Act 5, Scene 5, William Shakespeare

Lesson 16: Control is an illusion - always.

4 Stick a fork in front of me. I'm done.

Now what? Another corporation? A bigger title? A corner office? Nothing about any of those things held my interest. My kids were now independent and finding their own paths. Was I a good role model? I'd come a long way, right? Would my legacy now be simply surviving the corporarium?

No, this was my life! I needed to be creative and productive in an environment where my challenges were rhetorical, not political. I needed to put my abilities to the test in a broader environment. And I knew I had to do it before I was too burned out to care. This was my fork in the road.

I wanted my own voice back. I wanted (the illusion of) control. I wanted to do the right thing, not just what was dictated by my over-lords. I wanted something that could keep my brain stimulated for-ever; something that would allow me to work independently when I needed to, and indefinitely if I wanted to. There were no dreams of a life of leisure or retirement for this girl. I'm not wired that way.

Writing for people in different industries with different challenges was appealing on every level. The diversity would feed my curiosity, my wanderlust and the Muse that was now screaming to be heard.

Helping people communicate ideas is what I lived for. And who better than an impatient reader to write for an audience suffering with triage burns from information overload?

Was freelance copywriting a viable profession for me? I thought about the independent graphic designers, photographers and videographers I'd worked with for years. Autonomy was essential to them, and they willingly made sacrifices to keep it. They had inspired me more than I realized.

Why wouldn't it work for me too? People pay for writing. Would they understand the value I bring to them? If it turned out I was wrong, would I go back to the corporarium? No, this was my line in the sand.

Lesson 17: A girl's got to do what a girl's got to do.

Making a conscious decision to leave extremely gainful employment for artistic freedom does beg the question, what in Sam Hill are you doing? (I'm sure that's what my husband was thinking.) Even with temporary cash reserves to pay the bills while you start your business, it's scary. People tell me it's scary. Candidly, I was ready to explore the world on my terms no matter what the cost.

As I closed the door to the corporarium, a huge chapter in my life closed with it. I wondered if I'd ever be back. Looking back to my days at the newspaper and selling cars, it suddenly struck me how far I'd come. It had been sixteen years and five employers since I came back to Chicago.

I had mixed thoughts when I left the last company. Did I say goodbye to everyone? Did I remember to grab my South Park wrist support? But not once did I think I'd made a mistake. I was absolutely clear about that. Having burned myself out compulsively trying to meet the company's expectations, it was going to take a while for the pistons to stop their frantic chugging.

The first weeks at home I didn't do much of anything except decompress and look out my office window into the back yard. It just didn't register. My senses had been ignored for so long that I was numb. It was Indian summer, and I couldn't feel it. I opened the window to see if I could smell it or hear it. But I still felt like third person singular.

Lesson 18: Patience. Even weeds come back to life.

5 DBA me before I change my mind
-Years 1 and 2-

My first official client was my former boss. I continued to edit and approve the corporate messaging around the world, but this time from my home office with the squirrels playing outside my window. Without the commute and angst it was the perfect transition to self-employment.

Since I'd never started a one woman business before, I quickly established myself as a sole proprietor through an online legal service and home-printed some basic business cards lest anyone think me an imposter.

About the third week I finally heard the birds and smelled the leaves. This triggered thoughts about the yard, the earth, and the cosmos. By the fourth week I actually listened when I spoke to myself. Deprogramming was taking hold.

As much as I appreciated the work from that first client, it wouldn't sustain me forever. Within six months my old job was filled by some-one with his own connections, and the work dried up. Now it was time to put my old prospecting skills to the test. See? Those early detours we hate are just life classes we're forced to take for our own good. I remembered something my mentor told me. "Once you're on your own, you'll see opportunity everywhere." He was right.

Selling for my own business was extremely rewarding. I got lucky again. My previous manufacturer became a client. It was a match made in heaven. I knew the company, its products, its messaging and most of its marketing people. What's more, as my contacts moved on to other jobs, they brought me into their new companies.

Projects took me into change management messaging for multi-billion dollar corporations, video production, direct mail and web site content. I worked with Sales, Service, Marketing, HR and leadership teams across different industries. I felt I'd arrived.

Lesson 19: Remember what they say about burning bridges?

Not knowing what to predict for income that first year, I was just happy the number was going up. Graphic designers I had hired in corporate life became symbiotic partners which opened up more new clients for all of us. The collaborative nature of each project and a diverse assortment of companies gave me the satisfaction that I dreamed of when I became a freelancer. Why hadn't I done this before?

Someone was definitely watching over me. The fact that things were moving along with minimal drama was obviously proof that I had suf-fered enough. This was my reward. Obviously.

Lesson 20: If you think you've suffered enough, you are obviously delusional.

6 Help me. The dog ate my homework.
-Years 3 and 4-

With six steady clients and two solid subcontracting relationships functioning, and a dwindling supply of home-printed business cards, I decided it was time to invest in some branding. I still had no logo, no brochure, no brand identity, no swag, and no web site. Facebook was in its infancy. I really took my time building collateral. After all, it had to be an honest representation of me. Nothing was printed until I heard all the right bells going off in my head.

Two more clients joined me in the fourth year which effectively doubled my income over the year before. I now had a graphic identity I loved, a professional brochure and cards I was proud to hand out, and a need to find more hands to put them in. Enter the networking group.

It took some real convincing to get this commitment-phobe to pay to join a weekly early morning business networking group. But when I finally agreed to visit, I saw the benefits quite clearly, and enjoyed the members.

Fellow networkers helped me to see more outlets for my skills. They introduced me to their friends and clients creating more potential business. I got comfortable addressing a group. Looking at my client list today, I can trace over half back to introductions made by those very networkers.

I'm not saying that every minute spent networking was time well spent. It surely wasn't. I wasted many hours over coffee or wine with people that were not a good fit for my business. But it was a developmental step I needed to take. Socializing with other small business owners made me comfortable in all sorts of situations. It was good sharing many of the same frustrations too – cash flow, marketing plans, cash flow.

Lesson 21: Networking is better than not working.

-Years 5 through 7-

I got my first taste of statistical reality in year five. Though I tripled my new clients, the year's revenue growth was flat. Some of this I attributed to networking reciprocation from companies with small marketing budgets.

One of my friends was a business coach, so I cornered him. He was wonderfully human and listened patiently without passing judgment. Working with him gave me an evolving awareness of where I was and where I could go. He drew a circle on a piece of paper with a smaller circle inside it, and said, "This is you inside your business right now. "

He continued. "Lots of people don't want to stay there. Their vision is to move outside the circle, hire people to do the work, and manage the workers." He drew another circle with a small circle outside of it. Pointing to the smaller circle he asked, "Will this be you in five years?"

"No way," I said. "I don't want to manage people. I want to be the hands on worker in this scenario." Saying it out loud again felt right. Though from a business perspective, I knew he made a good point. So right then and there, in the middle of my fifth year of business, we wrote a business plan.

Lesson 22: Bass-ackward planning is better than none at all.

Year five was also the year I met the client from hell - the one who is late for meetings that he schedules, who contradicts himself daily, believes you are a faucet to be turned on at will, doesn't take the advice he requests, calls at all hours, and then complains about the invoice. I'm sure everyone who's run a business has endured this person. I, however, no longer do.

Knowing when a client is a liability is a tough call. And when building my business, I didn't want to say no to anyone. Partly it was about attaining critical mass. I knew there would be difficult clients, just like there are difficult coworkers, neighbors, and relatives. That's life. But the other 'partly' is that I was certain I could tame the wildest of beasts and still make money.

Here's a news flash. I am no tamer. I wanted to be. I thought I could keep my most difficult client happy without losing my mind. But the law of diminishing returns had other plans. Some working relationships are doomed. The harder I tried to placate the client, the less respect I got, and the less I respected myself. So the sooner I cut the cord, the sooner I could move on with clients that actually appreciated me. It was a good lesson.

Lesson 23: Sometimes you have to fire the client.

More disturbing news followed. By year six my active client base jumped by nearly thirty, though my revenue fell. It clearly showed me that while I had no trouble getting new clients, I wasn't acquiring clients with large projects. Was the dream over?

Not a chance. It was time to change my marketing strategy. I turned to one of my creative partners to help me build a website. I had put it off long enough. Since my business was 100% referral, I had postponed the investment. Now that it was done, I had a whole new attitude and a place to send people who wanted to see what my business was about.

In my sixth year two fellow networkers, each getting ready to publish their own books, asked me to do the editing. I was thrilled at the prospect of getting my big toe wet in the book publishing arena; and I was equally moved by the confidence the authors had in my abilities. Life was good.

Year seven I focused my energy on my strategic partners. Their clients needed help with larger content and messaging projects, and my clients needed their graphic/web/video talents. Projects got bigger and ran for longer time frames. The numbers didn't lie. Things were turning around.

Lesson 24: It's a lot easier to present yourself when you're presentable.

7 Shoot me or I'll jump.
-Years 8 to 10-

Sometimes I'm awash in deadlines; and other times it feels like everyone left earth and forgot to tell me that we were heading into a black hole. It's the nature of my business. But when the planets are properly aligned, clients bring wonderful, challenging opportunities to me, and all is right with the universe.

I watched the corporate pendulum swing from fully staffed marketing departments to independent contractors, and back, more than once. Many talented creatives found themselves suddenly out on the street frantically looking for a new place to call home before unemployment ran out. Those who went through it know that job security doesn't exist.

As a freelancer I didn't have to worry about being fired, just being paid. I loved hearing the mail truck move up the street. But when cash flow became critical, a trip to the mailbox felt like a replay of Schrodinger's cat: until you opened it, the possibility of a live check existed. Open it? Don't open it. Open it? Oh hell. So I invented a mailbox game for myself. If I opened the box and there was no check, I'd burst out laughing and say out loud, "Yes!" As ridiculous as that sounds, it kept me from screaming.

Not only is it hard to plan without definite paydays, it's a morale issue. Inevitably, the money arrives. But think about it. How would you react if you worked your two forty-hour weeks and on payday the company told you you'd get your check in two months? It doesn't matter how much money you have in the bank. Whatever the reason, not being compensated in a reasonable time feels a lot like disrespect.

Lesson 25: Many companies take 45-90 days (or more) to pay invoices.

There are occasional hiccups in the time space continuum of marketing projects, especially those that have an approval hierarchy that looks like ancestry.com. I know how frustrating it is for my clients to wait for each step to be Okayed before proceeding. They're as anxious as we are to finish the project. But the gears lock up once in a while. ..it happens.

Lesson 26: Remember the pipeline and keep it from being holey.

8 Mistake? Hardly ever.

No, I don't eat steak all the time; nor is my wardrobe couture. But I 'm an expert on wines (under $7). Sure, stalled projects throw a wrench in my plans sometimes. That doesn't make me a masochist. Don't forget. I'm living my dream.

People are always asking me if I'm happy working for myself, especially just before they head back into their offices knowing I'll be cruising down the road with the windows open and the radio blasting. If I had it to do all over again, would I still be a freelance writer? Maybe a better question is what would I pay (or sacrifice) for a chance to live my paradoxical dream?

I get what Dickens was talking about. It is the best of times. It is the worst of times. I am my own boss, but accountable to many. I have the freedom to pursue so many wonderful projects and experiences - the freedom to decide how and with whom I conduct business. But I never know exactly what's coming, so it's a little hard to plan. Every day is an adventure.

Writing original copy that I like and that's successful for my clients is one of the most satisfying jobs I could ever have imagined. Being well-compensated for it makes freelance writing the best of all possible occupations for me. When clients return with more work, I'm proud and humbled by their trust and the opportunity to help them by doing what I love. My relationships with the people I work for validate my decision to set off on my own.

Self-employment also allows me to fill the odd little left-over moments in the day with real life-affirming activities like feeding the birds, volunteering, writing poetry and cruising antique shops. I can scream or laugh out loud whenever I need to, take breaks to sing Motown in front of the mirror, and get to work in inappropriate t-shirts. On balance my feet are firmly on the ground even when they're on my desk covered in flip flops. What price would you put on that?

Jim Carrey once told a graduating class, "You can fail at what you don't want, so you might as well take a chance on doing what you love." If I still had my big corporate job, how different would my life look? There might be more money in the bank; but there would also be a giant hole where my life force used to be, and aching regret for not taking a chance.

Lesson 27: Jim Carrey is right.

9 Ever after

Oh, I 'm sorry. Did you think that was the end?

"Go on vacation? How could I **ever after** the last 3 wretched months?" Yes, sometimes amid the silver linings there are clouds disguised as giant birds that defecate on your head when you least expect it. Don't laugh. That actually happened to me crossing a field once. Metaphorically it happens in more insidious ways.

Printers wear out. Operating systems become extinct. Clients are laid off, or go on long holidays. Strikes close down businesses in mid-project. Hey, I don't like when the fates poop on my head, but it comes with the job.

What also comes with the job are the joys of helping a young company find its message and its voice; bringing personality to an outdated website; telling a story for someone that moves an audience; fine tuning difficult correspondence; scripting a memorable video; building a messaging platform; helping people be successful.

I'm constantly reminded that being my own boss is a gift. As another entrepreneur recently joked, "I've been at this for twelve years. I'm now officially unemployable." I know what he means.

Ever after is what comes next for as long as you live. Whatever it is, I want to make it count for more than a bank statement. What we do defines us. Happily ever after for me means becoming the full definition of me. With all the bumps in the road, up to and including keeping a revenue stream flowing during a recession, it's no expressway (though it sometimes takes a toll). Still, the surprising twists and turns are what make the yellow brick road magical.

Creating something original that brings value to my client, my community or my family is what motivates and rewards me most of all. The more I write, the more I love to write.

Looking back through the years to the day I started working for myself, I don't see dollar signs. I see the faces of all the people I've worked with; I hear a thousand ideas in the voices of my collaborators; and relive the thrill of inspiration and success. Had I not set off on my own, those faces and voices and successes would not exist for me. And I can't imagine my life without them.

When it comes right down to it, success for me has always come from taking a chance. Some of those chances seemed to fly in the face of reason at the time I took them; but there was always something inside of me that said 'this feels right.' I learned to trust that feeling.

You measure your success differently when you are the ruler of your destiny. Being a freelance writer feeds my soul. It also puts me up against the elements, the odds, and my own shortcomings every day. I'm still learning. And at the pace the world is changing, I expect to be doing a lot more learning. Every challenge I take and every person I work with connects me to the world in ways I never expected. And I own all of it - good times and bad. But best of all, I own my destiny.

Lesson 28: When the game is calling, go ahead; get in there and be the ball.

Dedication

This true story is dedicated with deep love and gratitude to Fred, whose love gives me wings; Mark, for his honest critiques, Lindsay, and Paul, for their hugs and humor; Grace and Max, for later; Fred and Noreen who never stop giving; Mom, and Sam, who never got to publish their books; Dad, who taught me about audacity; Lisa, who always lets me bounce ideas off of her; Mary Lee, who told me to stop talking and start writing; Joey, who just told me to stop talking; the eight great coauthors of this book; Rosemary, who planted the seed; the clients, bosses, mentors, strategic partners and friends that inspired, challenged, and believed in me, especially AF, BB, BM, DV, GN, J^2, K^2, LP,LR, MC, MV, MW, SB, SH, and WS; and to every woman who ever doubted herself.

Have brain. Will Storm.

Kathy Eber is a free-spirited content creator, scripter, editor, author, ghost writer, and muse who collaborates with businesses and individuals that have precious little time to spend creating original content and communications. She lives to find and fine tune the authentic message and voice in all her work. As one client put it, "she has no patience with mediocrity." Based in the Chicago area with her husband Fred, she writes for and collaborates with businesses across the country on projects from taglines and blogs to websites and video. Port Eber Communications opened its doors in 2004. Knock anytime. www.porteber.com

You can reach her at authorkathyeber@gmail.com

Out of Chaos Comes Clarity

By Michelle Prima, Professional Organizer

Write me a story.

I've always loved to write. What has that to do with organizing, you ask? Life has a tendency to come full circle. You'll see my point by the end of my story.

My love for writing began with my love for reading. My earliest recollection of books is sitting with my siblings on the sofa every evening, with our dad squeezed between us. We all dressed in our matching pajamas, and listened with rapt attention while he read from *The Arabian Nights*, *Black Beauty* and *Heidi*. These stories took us to faraway places, with the characters living lives we'd never see, or at least, we didn't think we'd ever see.

It wasn't until high school that I picked up my first historical romance, *The Flame and the Flower* by Kathleen Woodiwiss. I was hooked. I even started writing my own stories with friends, using characters from television, or creating my own. I guess we were writing "fan fiction" before the world of the internet. I stopped writing once in college. Homework seemed to take priority for some reason. Then I graduated, got married and had my daughters. I was too busy to do much writing. Funny how children will do that to you – eat up your time.

I was busy with my career, too. I'd received a bachelor's degree as a Registered Record Administrator, now called Health Information Management. I followed that up with a Master's Degree in Health Care Management. When I look back on this from an organizing standpoint, it makes perfect sense. After all, I enjoyed working in the hospital setting, but didn't want to deal directly with patients. Instead, I had the wonderful job of making sure all their forms were properly completed and signed, and their files stored neatly on shelves in the records room. I'd found my calling before I knew what my calling was.

The writing bug hit me again when my daughters were both in school. If you're a writer, you understand. Once exercised, though the gene may be dormant, it continually tries to fight its way out. Ideas flit through your brain, and stories slowly unfold, even if the words aren't put to page.

I'd stopped working by then, after realizing the cost of working and daycare nearly exceeded my income. I needed something to fill the time while they were gone for a few hours. Housework and I were never a good match. So I started dabbling in writing my own historical romances, and joined Romance Writers of America. I was also a member of the local Chicago-North chapter, where I met many others who shared my passion for reading and writing romance novels. But the industry was beginning to falter by then. It was more difficult to get published as houses merged and lines disappeared. And although I had an agent, nothing ever came of my manuscripts.

I kept writing, though. I'd surrounded myself with writer friends, and since I still had time on my hands, and needed a little income to support my writing efforts, I offered my web design services, such as they were, to my fellow authors. I'd done my own site already – a very primitive page before things like java and mp3 files existed. In fact, it still exists to this day. I really need to update it!

And so my first business was born – Literary Liaisons, Ltd. In addition to web site design, I self-published a Victorian Research manual and wrote some freelance articles for various magazines.

I also self-published a tips booklet targeting authors and writers called "101 Organizing Tips for Writers." Although this was written before the world of social media, many of the tips are timeless and still relevant.

Through it all, I kept in touch with the world of romance fiction, even as my real-life world was falling apart…

Did I really just do that?

I'd known for years I wasn't happy in my marriage. But how to walk away from it when I knew the consequences? I knew my daughters would suffer along with me. Was that fair? But was staying in an unhappy marriage any fairer to them?

I would have to say that this period of my life has been the most difficult so far; yes, even more challenging than starting, running and growing a business - probably because of the emotional drain. The emotional stresses affected my health, although I didn't know that was the cause at the time. I went through EKGs and EEGs and stress tests, all trying to pinpoint the cause of my symptoms. But nothing was ever diagnosed throughout these grueling months.

Luckily, I had a wonderful support group in my friends who helped me through the process and change. I couldn't have done it without them. They know who they are as they read this.

During this life shift, I met a man who kept me laughing and smiling, no matter what the world threw at me. That's not an easy task. But more important, he passed the porch test. What is the porch test? It's simple. Could I see myself as an old woman sitting on the porch with him, rocking slowly while the sun set? You bet! We married in June, 2004, doubling the size of our families.

And who would have guessed, but all those medical issues I'd been having? They went away when I settled in to my new, happier life.

From chaos comes clarity.

Backtrack a little to raising my daughters. During that time, I'd unfortunately let my continuing education credits lapse on my degree. I'd gone back to work, but as a Pharmacy Technician, yet another job requiring accuracy and discipline. More foreshadowing of my business-to-be.

While at the pharmacy, I'd come to the realization that a new career was in order. I could either catch up with years of continuing education credits, and pay and sit for the Health Information Management accreditation again. Or I could start something totally new to fit in with my new life. What that would be, I wasn't certain.

That's when I stumbled upon the NAPO (National Association of Professional Organizers) web site. That's when I learned that there were over 4000 men and women out there making a living by organizing other people. That's when I learned I could take my love of putting things in order and transfer my skills to others.

Thus was born my organizing business. But I wanted it to be more than that. So I played with different names. I wanted to use my last name, and I knew early on I didn't want to limit my business to organizing. I asked for feedback from friends. That gave birth to Prima By Design, Inc. I hired a lawyer to incorporate my business. I bought my domain name and designed my web site. I added phone and fax lines to my office. And I designed my logo with the help of my daughter.

How did my logo come to be? I chose my color scheme based on the bow atop a package she'd given me. I loved the combination of turquoise, navy and lime green. Was it an acceptable color scheme when it comes to marketing? I didn't really care because I liked it and it suited me. Sometimes you just have to do what you want for your business, not what the experts say.

Once I had the skeleton of my business, I started training. I knew how to organize, but I didn't know how to transfer those skills to others, or what marketing would work best, or what a contract should include. I joined NAPO National along with the local NAPO-Chicago chapter. I took online courses for running an organizing business and absorbed all I could from local veteran organizers.

But, like all new businesses, there was the challenge of building my client base. I started by doing some pro bono work in exchange for testimonials. My first client came as a referral from the NAPO web site. The job was an hour away, but she was my first paying client! I didn't care in the beginning. And she even referred me to her niece. Still, I wanted my client base closer to home, so I joined the local chamber of commerce.

I made a lot of business connections at the chamber. That's also where I found my first accountant. He sat with me and helped me set up my QuickBooks accounts correctly. I was grateful for the assistance, and after spending hours and hours on our tax returns that year, gladly handed it all over to him the following year. And while I still do all my own data entry with QuickBooks, I've learned to leave the important stuff like payroll and tax returns to the accounting professionals.

After joining the chamber, I was introduced to a professional networking group. It was through them that I learned not only good networking techniques, but also the power of referral marketing.

Added to my own client base, my business began to grow. I also revamped my web site and hired a business coach to take me to the next level. It was then that I began to branch out...

It's a dog, dog, dog, dog world.

If someone had told me forty years ago that I would be the owner of five dogs as an adult, I wouldn't have believed them. After all, my only visit to the Emergency Room as a child was when I'd had an asthma attack before I was a year old. The reason? It was an allergic reaction to my grandmother's dogs. I never had another attack, but I remember well into my thirties that any time I was around a dog, my eyes would begin to itch and water, I'd have sneezing attacks, and would get short of breath. As soon as I removed myself from the house, I'd be fine.

Yet, I still loved to be around dogs. I even wanted to be a veterinarian. But the allergies were too severe to pursue that career. Besides, life had other plans for me. Yet, dogs seemed to sense that I had affection for them, because they always wanted to be near me whenever I visited someone's home. And while I could tolerate them for a short while, I would soon have to shoo them away.

Over the years, the allergies seemed to ease, while allergies to cats became worse. But as much as my daughters wanted a dog while they were young, it wasn't to be, for a variety of reasons. My love for them never ceased, though. That's a good thing, because dogs have always been a part of my husband's life.

When we first started dating, his mastiff, Zeus, was living with a friend. Steve knew about my allergies, but wanted me to meet him anyway. We did a test since my allergies seemed to be under control. Could I spend a weekend with the dog without having an asthma attack? Luckily, I could. In fact, after taking some allergy medicine, I made it through the weekend with very few symptoms.

So it was settled, Zeus could come back home. But he was lonely and aging, so we added a puppy to the mix, a chocolate lab named Loki. It was a dog I'd always wanted. He was adorable, and kept Zeus on his toes, but was a typical lab – energetic, chewing on furniture, eating whatever was in sight.

Meanwhile, I was living with my youngest daughter and renting a house. It was just the two of us there, and my older daughter would come to spend weekends with us. One year Steve and I took all four of our children to the Chicagoland Pet Show, and then stopped at a local pet store on the way home. Everyone fell in love with an adorable Akita puppy. But I was a working mom, with little free time on my hands. And my landlord, while not forbidding pets, had rented to me with the knowledge that I didn't have a dog.

Needless to say, I was upset when Steve showed up on my doorstep one afternoon with the sweet little Akita we'd seen in the pet shop. I'd never owned a dog—with good reason. Would my allergies rear their ugly heads again if I were exposed to a dog 24/7? Plus, I knew nothing about raising them! They took up time and money I didn't really have. But he felt my daughters and I needed a guard dog; and there she was – all three month old soft, furry 'puppiness' of her. I was hooked. If you've ever owned an Akita, you know what I mean.

Loki and Bera were close in age – only six months apart. So they grew up together, loving each other's company. And when Steve and I married, they were happy to be living together. Zeus was still around, and kept them both in check in his passive, lazy way. Perhaps it was his sheer size. But whatever it was, they behaved for him…and us.

When they were both two years old, we learned of a family who needed to find a new home for their bloodhound because they didn't have time for him. Steve loves bloodhounds, so we paid a visit and picked him up. He was a real sweetheart, that Marley. I think he would have gone home with anyone (except his current owner).

As we spent more time with Marley, we learned more and more about him. It was soon evident that his last owners abused him. We had to re-teach him manners. No, you can't take the laundry from the hamper. No, you can't sit on Steve's favorite recliner. It was several months before he became a well-behaved dog. But what we didn't know was that he wasn't healthy. He suffered from allergies – lots of them. I didn't even know dogs, like humans, could have allergies. The poor boy spent the rest of his life on antihistamines, trying to keep his itchy skin at bay.

It was a few years later when we attended the pet expo again. This time, we saw a litter of seventeen lab/bloodhound puppies – all black as night, those blabs. Since Steve had a bloodhound, though not a typical bloodhound, we thought that raising one from a puppy would give him a real one. It turned out Raven is more lab than she is blood-hound. So much for that theory. But they bonded anyway, because Steve was home for over a year with a work-related injury.

Puppy made five dogs – Zeus, Loki, Bera, Marley and Raven. Don't tell the other dogs, but Bera, my Akita, is still my favorite. Maybe it's because she was my first. But probably it's because Akitas are adept at making their way into your heart. They are a very unique breed with their intelligence and antics; which is why I became a volunteer for the Midwest Akita Rescue Society. I've helped with transport and home checks, and also maintain their Owner/Shelter page on their web site. The stories break my heart sometimes. My dream is to one day be able to foster and save even more of them. But as long as I have my organizing business, the dogs will have to wait. I'm just thankful I have the flexibility of owning my business so I can devote time to MARS. Another perk of being the CEO!

Sadly, Zeus and Marley crossed the bridge after giving us more years than is usual. As Loki and Bera aged, we decided to buy a pure-bred bloodhound to keep Raven company. And so we have Belde – a goofy and loveable and leggy puppy from Louisiana. He's been a challenge with a dislocated hip and stroke within his first eleven months of life. But we wouldn't trade him for the world.

As I write this, Loki has crossed the bridge, too, after giving us many years of unconditional love. If someone had told me forty years ago that I'd be a nursemaid to these, our six dogs, I'd say they were crazy. But it seems I've fulfilled my dream to be a vet, albeit an in-home one.

All the homes are a stage.

After attending my first NAPO conference, I learned that the industry isn't just about organizing. There were so many opportunities out there…so many specialties. One of those that really interested me was Home Staging. Perhaps it was my creative side calling to me, but I loved the idea of walking into a home and making it ready to sell.

So I looked into different programs and signed up for a 5-day class with the Midwest Staging Redesign Institute. It was a very small class – just me! So I had the full attention of the instructors, and probably learned more than I would have in a larger class. The best part was the hands-on exercise and final exam. I walked into a home that was on the market, but not occupied. The instructors had piled all the accessories in one room, pushed all the furniture to the middle of the rooms, and let me at it!

It's amazing how much there is to consider when placing furniture in a room – lighting, conversation, focal points, traffic patterns. Accessories can really add or detract from any of these. The home was an empty slate, and it was fun painting the picture.

I also practiced on an occupied home, using the items the homeowner already had. I de-cluttered and rearranged the furniture. Redesign is a much different technique, because the furniture isn't always best for the space. It's the designer's job to make it look like it fits the room.

Included in the class were marketing materials. I was allowed to use them with my own logo. So I created brochures and fliers, and began marketing to real estate brokers and home sellers. My business name already encompassed the additional services I'd be offering. That had always been part of the plan—one that includes more than just organizing. The best part about the job was buying accessories for use in staged homes, especially the empty ones. Sometimes, a trio of candlesticks or a cookbook propped on the kitchen counter is just enough to create an illusion for the potential buyers.

Then the real estate industry collapsed…

Let me tell you about your closet.

It was a few years into my business when I saw an advertisement in the NAPO Chicago newsletter for an opening as a sales representative at a local family-owned closet design company. My client base was solid, but stagnant, and staging jobs were few and far between because of the state of the industry. So I inquired into the position. After two interviews, I was offered the job.

Training was more intense than I thought it would be. I had no idea how involved the process was. I learned about closet types, typical layouts, and measuring to the ¼ inch. I learned about the challenges of working around piles of clothes, construction dust and price shoppers. And I learned about wood laminates, wood veneers, drawer slides and door hardware.

I went with a senior designer on a few appointments for on-site training. She showed me how to hold the measuring tape (yes, there's an art to that), how to design on the fly, and how to sell the design and negotiate the price.

The biggest challenge? Learning the software program. The company gave me my own laptop, but I had never used CAD software. Drawing lines to the exact length, adding text boxes, dropping in all the closet components from the libraries…it was a learning curve…a very slow one. But after a while, it was fun. The colors and 3D renditions were fun to generate.

Once I mastered the software, designing and pricing, I was on my own. It was a great experience. I was able to bring my organizing skills to the job, planning out the best place for shoes or how much long hang vs. short hang was needed. I could discuss these ideas with the homeowners from an organizer's standpoint as well as a closet designer's.

As a company, we had monthly staff meetings where we discussed new products and challenges we faced. Luckily, I made my own schedule, so I could still fit in my organizing clients.

But after a couple of years, I began to realize that I couldn't give either job 100%. And organizing was my true calling. So I said good-bye to the closet company. I don't regret my time with them. I learned a lot about the closet industry, and can intelligently discuss closet design and products with my organizing clients to this day.

A crease in the paper

About five years into my business my husband injured himself at work (twice) and missed a year and a half of work because of the injuries, surgeries and recovery. It was a Worker's Comp case, so we weren't left destitute, but finances were a little tight. The case didn't settle for five years.

My business was still steady, but not growing by leaps and bounds. I'd taken on a new client, a chiropractor, through my network. I started by organizing the office space. I looked at work flow, layout, etc., and set up systems to help the staff run a smooth operation.

This job also had a unique challenge – that of HIPAA and confidentiality. How to keep information and records confidential in an open office space? Luckily, I was able to draw on my background that I never thought I'd use again – my degree in record administration. I knew this stuff. I knew we couldn't discuss patients with other visitors or use last names when talking to them in the open. Records had to be kept locked up at night and software had to be secure.

I was in my element again.

The office went through several moves, and I was there for each one, helping design spaces and manage work flow. I'd also been given the task of accounting—keeping track of financial records, paying bills and entering hours for payroll.

Eventually, I became one of those 'payroll' entries. As the office enlarged, so did the need for my time. There were policies and procedures to write, supplies to order, financial reports to run and schedules to coordinate. So I joined the payroll, eventually working almost 30 hours/week. It was nice to have steady income, while still having the flexibility of my business.

The Open House at the new facility was the pinnacle of our success. Business associates showed up to tour the facility and enjoy the refreshments. Even the chamber president was there to help cut the ribbon. We also held a bowling afternoon for the patients.

As the months went by, patients came and went. I continued in my tasks, and it was a joy to greet patients and help out at the front desk. Then suddenly, the office turned upside down.

In just a few weeks, personal issues intruded upon the owner's life. And while she struggled to handle them, the office imploded for a variety of reasons. In January of 2011, I found myself unemployed.

It was devastating, of course. I'd never been let go from a job. And the reasons were ridiculous. Me, uncooperative and disruptive? Describe me thusly to my other clients, and they just shake their heads in wonder. But it was all part of the instability of the office and owner. I didn't take it personally. And as I look back, it was the best thing that ever happened to me. Why? Because it gave me a swift kick in the rear.

I knew that if I wanted to make my business succeed, I needed to dedicate 100% to it. No more part-time jobs. I needed to make a serious effort of marketing and networking if I wanted to be truly self-employed in a viable business.

It was then that I found my old network again. I joined a lunch group in Palatine. It was the best investment I made. I volunteered for leadership positions over time, which helped establish my credibility and visibility within the chapter. It didn't take long for referrals to start coming in. Some were short-term, others are on-going.

I also started attending more NAPO Chicago meetings. I contacted libraries and other organizations for speaking opportunities. I interviewed with local newspapers and submitted articles to local magazines.

Then I jumped into the Social Media fray. I started a blog, created a Facebook page for my business, and joined Twitter and Pinterest. It was fun at first. But I really wonder how anyone keeps up with all the posts and re-tweets and hash tags and favorites. I've pulled back some, but remain active. I now have a monthly newsletter. I post on

Facebook daily, and I check Twitter and Pinterest occasionally. My clients are more important to me than how many 'likes' I get.

Turning the page on age...

Over 10,000 people age into Medicare every day. Some of them are still working. Some are retiring. Some have already retired. And still others are downsizing now that the nest is empty. That brings with it a whole new market to organize and serve – seniors.

But seniors are also a special market. They often have physical challenges, whether it's limitations in their mobility or in their mental capacity. While most of them are quite capable of giving directions to their helpers, there are some who have to rely on family members to direct matters. Adding family to the mix often creates new problems.

Wanting to work with seniors, I trained with eSMMART, and became a Certified Senior Move Manager. In this class, I learned that the senior is my client. If there are conflicting directions from the senior and family members, I must listen to the senior. It is not my job to intervene and go against my client's wishes because the family wants it a certain way.

Downsizing is a step most seniors go through during their lives. It became my job to help them through the process. I look at the new space with them, and determine which of their belongings are necessary in their new home. Once that is determined, I help them decide what else they would like to bring with them.

We start with the basics – bed, dresser, kitchen table and chairs. Then we add those personal touches of family photos and curio cabinets. If they are moving from a three-bedroom house with basement into a one bedroom apartment, you can imagine how much is left over. It is usually the wish of the senior for the family to take what they want before disposing of the extra furniture and belongings. Once that's done, it's my job to find outlets for the rest of the belongings.

In most instances, the house is being sold. So, drawing on my staging experience, I use some of the pieces left in the house to stage the home before it goes on the market. After the house sells, the remainder of the items needs to be disbursed. That may mean selling them or donating them. It is the client's decision. I pull from my vast resources to find the most economical solution for the client.

The final task is to help the senior settle into the new home. Because it's usually smaller, my skills as an organizer are well-utilized. I look at cabinet space and closet space. I look at products that will maximize small spaces. Most of the time, everything fits nicely. But there are those instances where the senior needs to purge just a little bit more.

This is just one way I can help seniors. Many no longer drive, so I run errands like grocery shopping, or taking them to doctor appointments. There are those that need nothing more than organizing. I use the same approach with them as I do with the rest of my clients, though sometimes working in shorter sessions. I leave it up to them.

Write me a story redux.

So remember at the beginning of my story when I said my love for writing came from reading? Well, here's where life comes full circle.

I've always loved to read, and while a paperback feels great in my hands, I am sort of getting used to reading on a tablet when I travel. And I've never lost my love for writing.

I'm always finding ways to incorporate that skill into my business.

I started with my web site. I added an article every month as informational pieces. Then I started putting these articles into a monthly newsletter. I kept adding content to my newsletter, and changing the format through the years. I still send it out monthly, with a main article, a product recommendation, tips and fun facts.

When I was laid off from the chiropractor's office, I started posting on Facebook. I had a different theme every month, and posted a tip for that theme. I also started a blog. I was writing a post a day, but that quickly became too time-consuming. So I went down to once/week. I'm not always on schedule, but that's okay, because my clients come first.

And some of those clients have hired me to do their newsletters. I've managed to incorporate my writing skills into my business and get paid for it. Some clients provide me with their content, and I edit it and format it, then send out the newsletter. Some clients want me to write the content. It all depends on their comfort level with writing. For those who write their own content, it's both a technical and time issue. These clients are mostly published authors. So they would rather spend their time on manuscripts than trying to figure out the nuances of formatting and publishing a newsletter.

In addition to helping authors with their newsletters, I also provide virtual assistant services for them. Some ship me copies of their books for contests and giveaways. Some send me bookmarks for shipping. Some have me keep their web sites updated.

Yes, I've come full circle, and kept my world of writing close to my business and my heart. Will I ever be published in fiction? We'll see where life takes me. As I write this short story of my long life, I've had some real eye-openers.

Would I do it all the same way if I were to start over? No, I wouldn't. But I don't regret the path I've taken. The mistakes and side-steps have taught me some invaluable lessons.

As I look back, I also ask myself, have I really done all this? After all, it's only the tip of the iceberg of my life. I never thought I'd faced so many adversities, perhaps because everything always turned out for the best.

I never really thought of my life as adventurous, or myself as amazing. But after putting it all down on paper, I'm proud to leave this legacy that is me to my children.

About Michelle Prima

Michelle Prima has been organizing homes and offices since January 2005, when she started Prima By Design, Inc, located in Buffalo Grove, IL. She offers organizing, relocation, virtual assistant and errand services. Michelle has a bachelor's degree in Health Information Management, a Master's Degree in Health Care Management, and has worked in both hospital and retail settings.

Always organized, she trained professionally with members of NAPO (National Association of Professional Organizers), the Midwest Staging Redesign Institute and eSMMART. She is a Certified Staging Professional and a Certified Senior Move Manager. Professional memberships include NAPO, NAPO Chicago, NAPO Golden Circle and Business Network International. In her spare time, she does volunteer work for the Midwest Akita Rescue Society.

Connect with Michelle:
847-955-1822
michelle@primabydesign.com
www.primabydesign.com
Facebook.com/primabydesign
Twitter.com/MichellePrima13
primabydesign.blogspot.com/
theorganizedwriter.blogspot.com/

I Never Planned This

By Kari Skloot, Life-Work Coach/Consultant

I never needed to plan

I'd like to tell you that I always wanted to own my own business. I'd like to say it was the result of excellent planning and careful thought. But I can't. The truth is I never planned it at all.

Even as a first-born, I've never really planned much of anything in my life. Things really always came pretty easy for me. I was the girl in middle school who always got straight A's without really trying. I always sat first-chair in band even though I didn't practice my saxophone every night like I should have. Teachers seemed to like me a lot and I had friends. It was the same in high school. Straight A's, first chair in band and jazz band, and Varsity cheerleader.

I never got the romantic lead in the school musicals, but I always played the second lead which was the comedic role which meant I got all the laughs. I always had boyfriends and wonderful boyfriends at that. I ran with the popular crowd, the band crowd and the brainy crowd; I seemed to fit from one group into another pretty easily. I never had to plan or really try too hard to get anything I wanted. Good things just seemed to happen. Kind of sickening, right?

Into a man's world of trucking

My charmed life followed me into college, with just a few hiccups. I received academic scholarships and went to the same university as my high school boyfriend. My passion for being on stage and center of attention was fulfilled when I was cast in "Grease" as a freshman. I didn't really use that to launch anything, but it was a fabulous experience.

As a junior in college, I finally had to get serious and pick a major. I had started college on a math / science teacher scholarship, but I left that program when I realized I just wasn't that interested in teaching. Next I had tried being a theater major. I was good, but "good" isn't enough to make it in the world of theater. So, what was I supposed to do?

I wish I could say that I selected my major because I felt passionate about the subject or that I thought I was really good at it. Truth is I picked it because it was unique – because there were only four women who had selected that as a major, so I would stand out and be the center of attention. I wanted to be noticed and to rule the world. Yep – my degree is in transportation / logistics. Don't get me wrong, I found it very interesting, and I still do, but it never was my passion. I simply wanted to be noticed.

Introduction to female mentors

My first job out of college took me to Charlotte, North Carolina to work for a trucking company. Didn't plan on leaving the Midwest, but I thought, "What the hell!" I think if you're young and get the opportunity to live someplace else, you should. True to my desire to be noticed and to be first, I was the first woman to ever go through their management training program.

During training, I learned to drive a semi. However, I was so bad at driving it that out of the four of us in the class, I was the only one who wasn't allowed to take the truck out of the parking lot at Lambeau Field! Wise decision. After a few short months, I realized that I wanted to stay in the Midwest so, I moved to the Chicago area where my husband had been raised.

Once in Chicago, I was hired in the warehouse department of an auto glass company as an inventory specialist. Shortly into that job, a position opened to run the office of a small subsidiary the company was purchasing. Again, I took a chance. As with 99.9% of the chances I've taken in my career, it was a good pay-off. I learned a great deal about running a small business because, even though it was technically a division of a larger corporation, it was run very much as a small business model with personalized customer service. I had a lot of freedom to make decisions and make an impact. In a little more than a year, I was offered a promotion to the finance department at the corporate offices. I jumped at this chance. Nothing like I'd ever done before, but it was an opportunity I couldn't say no to. And, this was the first time I ever had a female boss.

In an ideal world, having a female boss should not be any different than a male boss. But we live in the real world. I immediately noticed the difference. These women were working in a male-dominated industry, but exuded such confidence that you could almost feel the power aura around them. Never once did I get the dreaded "she-devil" boss, just support and trust that I would do the job they were asking.

Deb taught me how to lead with patience and compassion. She was available, yet expected that I could find solutions myself. She knew I was smart enough to do the job I was hired to do, yet compassionate enough to help and really teach me when I needed it. Our director, Sharon, was cut from the same cloth. I consider her my first real mentor. She got noticed and commanded a room without overpowering it; a delicate balance – almost an art. This was the first time I ever aspired to move ahead in my career. I wanted to be like Sharon: smart, confident, encouraging and powerful. For a moment, I almost put a career plan in place! But then "life happened."

A club I never wanted to join

While I've never been one to plan (has driven my mother simply bonkers my whole life), I had *always* planned to be a parent. Well, as the saying goes, "the best laid plans of mice and men often go awry."

I was about 8 weeks pregnant when I started to hemorrhage at work right there in my cubicle, on the 18th floor of a building in the Loop in downtown Chicago. I will never understand why they bring fire trucks with ambulances when the emergency is clearly not fire related. My poor husband got to the building just in time to see the paramedics load me into the ambulance. Unfortunately, this was just my first miscarriage.

Fortunately, my two bosses were fabulous. As personal as the situation was, it had happened at work, so it was also a work thing. This was before people regularly worked from home (early 1990's), but they let me bring home anything I needed to keep on top of my responsibilities until I felt I was ready to come back to the office. They both led with such compassion and understanding that I have since adapted one of Sharon's sayings. "Work is work. But life happens."

It wasn't long after my second miscarriage (no ambulance ride this time) that I finally decided I was too nervous to continue working and commuting by train downtown. What if the next miscarriage happened on the train? Besides, by this time we were seeing a fertility specialist in the suburbs, and scheduling appointments was very challenging. So my infertility caused my job change.

After the wonderful and supportive experiences I had with female bosses, I actually considered the state of female leadership during my job search before I joined a third-party logistics company as a financial analyst. I was back fully in my college major, which most people find to be funny. Who works in their major? And it was led by a strong, smart, powerful woman. I was living the feminist dream!

Everywhere I looked in this company, there were women in power: the CEO, managers in the warehouses, department directors, and vice presidents. There was energy, creativity, cooperative discussion. Best of all, however, was the inherent power that each employee had – the right to challenge decisions and to ask questions. I can't say for sure if this is because the CEO was female, but I latched on to that freedom and ran with it.

I had no trouble finding suitable female mentors in this company. In fact, I had two while I was there: a VP of Sales and a VP of Marketing & Communications. They could not have been more different. Mary was the consummate sales professional; always looking for the "win-win." She entered every conversation with the firm belief that you can always find a compromise. She taught me to listen in a different way; to listen to the underlying message, not just what a person is saying. I also learned that a single conversation or transaction is not enough. I know it's a cliché, but this is where I first heard – and learned - "it's about relationships."

With Mary's support, I began working more and more with the clients. My confidence grew, and I realized that as good as I was with numbers, I was better with customer relationships. I presented my idea up the chain to take each of the large accounts that spanned multiple facilities and align them into a national accounts program. This is common now, but it wasn't in the logistics field in the 90's. While the account managers were still directly supervised by their local warehouse managers, I now led the multi-billion dollar program, soon took on my own national accounts and brought account managers into the corporate office. I was managing staff for the first time. Here's where Cheryl stepped in.

Cheryl was a free-spirit and contract VP of Marketing and Communications. She was interesting to a fault; I could listen to stories about her life and career all day long! She was a college professor, artist, basketball junkie, mother and marketing guru. I wanted to be Cheryl when I grew up. She hadn't "managed" her career – she just let it happen. And it worked for her. I knew now that it would continue to work for me, too. She gave me even more opportunities. She tossed "marketing" under my responsibility, and allowed me to incorporate marketing into our existing account relationships, not just for new businesses.

From Cheryl I learned that you don't have to necessarily know how to do the tasks to effectively manage the staff. I didn't know the first thing about graphic design, yet I was able to manage our graphic designers very successfully. She helped me take all the skills I had learned from my other work experiences and tie them into my own personal leadership style. She guided me through the process of coaching my team, rather than just supervising. And she opened up the world of "creativity" outside of artistic expression. I had never considered myself to be creative – I couldn't draw, couldn't paint, didn't do crafts – yet she helped me realize that I could still be "creative" just by thinking of something new and unique, by putting a framework around it or a loose structure through it. That was creative - strong, female and creative in the world of business.

A whole new world

I was now dangerously close to "planning" my career in this company. I loved what I was doing. I had freedom. I was confident enough to turn down the chance to be the account manager for our largest account because I personally didn't feel I could work with a tobacco company. There was so much support in this organization, that I never felt pressured or punished for my decisions. And I knew if I made a mistake because I took a creative chance, as long as I could defend the choice, I would still have my job. I accompanied the CEO on two trips to attend workshops led by Peter Drucker himself. I was being groomed for the next level. I was thriving. And then, life happened.

While working for this company, in fact right from the beginning, I experienced more reproductive issues. I turned 30 on a Friday, started with this company the next Monday, and miscarried that next Thursday. My fourth day on the job I had to ask for a "sick day." It was an inauspicious start. But as I said, I got nothing but support. During this timeframe, we also amped up our treatment for infertility. If you're not familiar with the infertility hamster wheel, it's one appointment after another: blood draws, ultrasounds, pills, and needles. Your entire schedule is built around your menstrual cycle – that is, the artificially managed menstrual cycle. After another round of in-vitro fertilization, we had achieved a pregnancy only to lose yet another one through a miscarriage.

Meanwhile, my husband and I joined a nonprofit organization called RESOLVE: The National Infertility Association. We went to nearly all the educational meetings and workshops. It was before most people were on the Internet, so meetings and communications were face-to-face. Soon I joined the board of the Illinois chapter. I was intensely passionate about this organization. I led workshops, scheduled educational programming, became the treasurer, managed the symposium, was interviewed for TV and newspaper, and before I knew it, became the president of the chapter.

We finally decided after six years that we could no longer go through with the IVFs. They were too hard on my body; and, for some unexplainable reason, I could not carry a pregnancy past 10-12 weeks. After much soul-searching and late-night discussions, we realized that adoption was the best route for us to build our family, and we fully embraced everything that would mean.

Unexpected twist

1999 was the year my career - and my life - took a dramatic turn. On January 2, 1999, during an incredible snowstorm, I received a phone call from a 16-year-old girl who was pregnant and hoping my husband and I would adopt her baby. Wow! We talked at least once a week every single week – even travelled to another state to meet with her a couple times. We hadn't planned on things happening so quickly. I mean we hadn't even gone through the licensing process nor had we picked an agency to work with! (I'll complain about the indignity of making prospective adoptive parents get a state license in my next book).

Nope, we hadn't planned, but that was nothing new for me. We scrambled to find an agency that would work with our out-of-state birth mother. We rushed through the licensing process as fast as possible, and selected an attorney. Within a few months, we were all ready to bring home a little boy and become parents. Again, the best laid plans...

I will not fault "Sue" for choosing to parent her baby. It seems almost unimaginable to me that any woman, let alone a 16-year-old girl, could make such a selfless and brave decision to place her baby with another family. I do believe it was her absolute intent, her plan, that we would be his parents. We sat with her and with the baby in the hospital the day after he was born. We talked, we laughed, we took pictures, we cried and we planned. It was going to be an open adoption, so we planned how we would make that work. We

I NEVER PLANNED THIS ⤳

were all set to pick him up and bring him home from the hospital that next morning. But the phone call we received wasn't the call we expected.

The next several months are a blur. I was devastated. My husband was devastated. My parents, my husband's parents, our family and friends had all planned that we would have a baby. But we didn't.

True to form, the company I worked for was wonderful. I was given as much time off as I needed, regardless of the days off I had earned. Everyone knew I had gone out of state to pick up my baby; so news spread quickly when it fell apart. I was grateful that I didn't have to tell the story. Thankfully, my boss shared the news before I returned. But when I came back to work, everything about me was different.

I had great difficulty keeping focused at work no matter how much I tried. I was still effective, but my heart wasn't in it. I must have been keeping it hidden well, because less than three months after I returned to work, the CEO offered me a new position. In fact, she was creating a new position for me – VP of Customer Innovations. I could become a leader in this company that had given me so much. I was going to have a real impact. But I just couldn't take it. My head was telling me that I should take advantage of this incredible opportunity. It was an absolutely perfect job custom made for me. But I continued to say no. My gut was telling me no. Something in those last three months had changed me fundamentally and irrevocably. Believe me, I never planned it.

First taste of non-profit

Next I made what could be a career-killing move, and left a seemingly perfect opportunity with a great company. I still have friends and family, more than 15 years later, who think I was insane for walking away.

But my heart had been ripped open. I was raw and vulnerable and suddenly consumed by emotions I had never felt. I just knew in my gut that I needed to focus on something more meaningful, and to focus on me. Yes, it was a rash decision. Yes, it was ill-advised. (The person who ended up taking that job is a very high-paid executive right now). Like most things in my career, this wasn't planned. It just felt "right."

So, here I was, devoting my time to my volunteer work with RESOLVE and making no money. Keep in mind that at this time I was the president of the board and we had just hired an executive director. My husband and I were in marriage counseling to try to deal with the devastating toll the failed adoption was having on our marriage. And then, opportunity knocked.

The executive director for the agency was not working out, so the board decided to let her go and began yet another search. One of my friends suggested that this time I throw my hat into the ring. Why not? I hadn't planned it, but we weren't finding anyone during the job search that seemed like the right fit. This might be a good idea. So, I resigned as board president and became the executive director for the Illinois Chapter of RESOLVE: The National Infertility Association.

I was now officially working in the non-profit sector! It was a part-time job, with an even more "part-time" paycheck. I had been making very good money in the corporate world, and this was just a drop in the bucket. Definitely a culture shock. But I felt comfortable and at peace. As corny as it sounds, I loved making a difference.

I was passionate about the mission of RESOLVE – to help people who were unable to have a child with their chosen partner to either become parents or to live a fulfilling life without parenting. The medical technology helping people create families was fascinating and continues to be even more so. The legal ramifications of that technology are beyond comprehension of most people. My heart was really aligned with this work.

Best job ever

A few months into my new role, I literally bumped into the greatest happening of my life. As executive director, I made it a point to attend all the educational programs our volunteers and partners presented. I wanted to talk to our members and support them in their journey. I needed to stay close with our partners and volunteers. Plus, I needed to stay on top of what was happening in the field of infertility.

After one such workshop on the topic of adoption, I was in the back of the room chatting with participants, when I accidentally bumped into the adoption attorney we had worked with during our failed adoption the prior year. As I apologized for knocking into her, she admitted she had been thinking about us. She seldom tells people what she does for a living because she finds it a bit uncomfortable when strangers ask her about ethics and legality of some family-building practices. A few days prior, however, her cleaning lady asked exactly what kind of law she practiced and for some reason, she told her. This woman instantly became emotional and shared that she had a friend through her church whose daughter was making an adoption plan for her baby, but had become less and less comfortable with the couple she had chosen. The attorney immediately thought of us.

We jumped at the chance. Totally unplanned, miraculously five weeks later we brought home our son. (In the next book, I'll tell you the wild story of our adoption – hospital workers putting up barriers, calls to State Senators and US Congressmen, calls to the governor's office, a husband in Singapore, a mad dash to the hospital and a man in a dress!) Best day of my life. Planned or unplanned, this boy was absolutely meant to be our son. I am connected to him on a level I still cannot fully comprehend. This is what my heart needed.

After taking off a few short weeks, I continued working part time for RESOLVE. I considered myself a full-time mom and part-time executive director. I ran this chapter out of the spare bedroom in my house while my son slept and when I could grab a few extra minutes. Don't ever let anyone tell you that "Parent" is not a career!

We were a small organization that was part of a larger national organization; so many larger decisions were handled at the national level. As technology started to change the way we operated, we found that fewer people were looking for face-to-face experiences like support groups and educational workshops. People were visiting chat rooms and searching for information on the internet. Doctors, egg donor agencies, surrogacy matching services and attorneys all were developing educational sections on their websites. Things were changing in our field, and RESOLVE needed to keep up.

Because I have a knack for seeing the big picture while looking at the details, I was asked to sit on a national team to chart the future of the organization as a whole. We all soon realized that we needed to move from a local chapter-based organization to a national organization with satellite service areas. So basically I reorganized myself right out of my job!

The biggest and the best

What would I do next? True to form, I didn't have a plan. My own personal experience with infertility had fed my passion to work for RESOLVE, and I didn't know how to identify that next passion. Because of that organization and our shared experiences, I had made many new friends. Two of those friends, who had both also become parents through adoption, were active with Relay For Life and the American Cancer Society. Knowing I had recently lost my father-in-law, relatives and other loved ones to cancer, they suggested I apply for an opening in the local office. This was a cause I definitely felt passionate about. I jumped at the chance… and I was offered the job.

Once again, I was lucky enough to be surrounded by incredible women. But this time, not only did I have strong female bosses, but also amazing female colleagues, peers, and employees. The office I worked in was all women (until the last 2 years), so the interpersonal dynamics were unlike any I had ever encountered before. Now I was sharing space and spending more than twelve hours a day with estrogen. Were there conflicts? Of course. Did everyone in the office get along? Of course not. But the energy and the unique passion were palpable. I saw the power of people truly passionate about saving each and every life affected by cancer. And I saw the tears and raw emotions when someone lost that battle. I have never cried as much as I did while working for the American Cancer Society.

My first direct boss, Carol, was in an interim role when I was hired. She was programming and I was fundraising, so we approached situations from entirely different perspectives. It made us a strong team; I like to think we worked better because of that. And I was blessed to have a team of people who were amazing at what they did. I once again had a charmed life. I had the dream job working for the biggest and the best non-profit in the world…and fighting cancer. What more could I want?

Once again, life happened.

Shortly after my first anniversary with ACS, I became very ill. I passed out during several work meetings and had to leave the office more than once in an ambulance. I am so grateful for my coworkers and friends who rode with me in those ambulances and stayed with me in the ER until my husband could arrive.

After a couple of months of tests, of touring all the ERs and hospitals in a 40-mile radius, I first had my gall bladder removed and then I was diagnosed with breast cancer. Fortunately, they caught mine so early that my oncologist told me some labs would have staged it at a 1 and some would have called it pre-cancerous. Regardless of the technicality of an exact stage, he told me that the plan and treatment would be the same: lumpectomy followed by five years on Tamoxifen. I am so grateful that I did not have to endure chemo or radiation. I am truly one of the lucky ones.

During this time, my team at work was incredibly supportive sending notes, flowers, and allowing me the extra time I needed to heal fully. Sometime after I returned, however, things began to change. I wish I could point my finger at one specific happening that changed it all for me. But in retrospect I think it was a confluence of everything falling at the same time.

The economy tanked, which meant donations were down substantially. In fact, for the very first time in my career, I had failed to make a goal. The people on my team were stressed out from the extremely long and hard hours demanded as event managers. People in the office were leaving for new positions. Volunteers were stressed and quitting. My boss had more responsibility added to her plate, which meant we had less time together as a team. Changes were happening in the entire organization.

Expectations of performance and output were raised to the point that I regularly worked 16-hour days. I no longer saw my child other than early mornings. I missed dinners, bedtimes, parties, family events and even weekends. And I was exhausted – physically and emotionally. This was not working any more. So without any plan for "what's next" I walked away. Yep, I left the biggest and the best "dream job" and I didn't have any job to replace it.

Refocus — again — on being a strong woman

Irrational and impulsive, yes. Empowering and healing, yes. I learned so much about myself during the next six months. I had to really think about what I wanted in a career and what I didn't. I know it sounds "hippie," but I really found myself. I asked the tough questions. I looked at what my skills were. What excited and energized me. And I accepted the fact that life happens. I made a positive decision to put myself and my family first. So yes, it was extremely empowering, and extremely frightening.

Now I was entering a new phase. I was unemployed, but by choice. I don't think I did anything but sleep the first four weeks. I was completely and utterly exhausted by any possible definition.

My close friends and family were incredibly supportive. They told me they admired me for putting myself and my health first. They told me they envied me for taking the leap. Not once did anyone call me an idiot – at least not to my face. But my self-esteem was shot. What kind of person walks out on a dream job? What kind of person can't handle the stress? What kind of person cuts her family's income by more than one third?

I needed to snap out of it. So I slowly began to rebuild my self-esteem, which at this point was intertwined with my career. I joined a career coaching group. I attended workshops. I networked face-to-face and on LinkedIn. I developed new friendships with fascinating people – women mostly. And slowly, I put on a happy face. I forced myself to get out of the house each day, even if it was just a quick run to the grocery store. At the very least, I had to shower and get dressed. I had to see other humans. I re-connected. I had "phone dates" with former colleagues. I met girlfriends for lunch and for coffee.

It took some time and some "faking it." But eventually I had to ask myself: what do I want to do next? What is my passion? Searching for a job is daunting for anyone; but for someone like me who doesn't plan, it's downright paralyzing.

A women's issue

Even doing all the job-search by the book (everyone says that networking is key), I found my next opportunity by answering a job posting with absolutely no connection or introduction. Leave it to me to find a different path.

The interview for Women's Health Foundation was one of the most unique interviewing processes I've ever experienced. Mind you, this is a very small agency with only a half-dozen employees who all work together in an open loft-type area. No privacy and very collaborative, so the interview was a full-on group activity. I absolutely fell in love with these women, and with the mission.

You don't really know how important and critical your pelvic health is until something goes wrong. Once is does, it impacts your entire well-being. Your pelvic floor is literally holding up everything. And there is absolutely nothing funny at all about peeing when you sneeze or lift something. I learned that there are excellent options! Who knew? Here I was raising funds for this little-known agency that unbeknownst to me, was making an incredible difference in the lives of women and girls. Yes, I could be passionate about this, too!

This group was the ultimate in strong female energy right to the core. Each woman who worked there was amazing. They supported one another wholly, both work and personally. Dogs were welcomed, and for a while there was even a bassinette for Colleen's little sweetheart. They were freakishly smart - some of the most brilliant women I've ever met! Hugs and hard work, but can't forget marguerita Mondays and wine Wednesdays. To this day, I can honestly say I've never loved working any place more than I loved working for Women's Health Foundation. Missy, you built an amazing team and I am simply honored to have been a part of it for even a short time. I felt valued and successful, which was exactly what I needed after being out of work for six months.

Unfortunately, once again - you know - life came knocking.

This time, however, it wasn't anything related to my health. The agency was reorganizing and cuts had to be made. I was one of three let go in a very short time period. Wow. I had never been let go before. The other times I was out of work had been my choice. This was something new and I was heartbroken.

A mission of safety

Fortunately, this time around I was only unemployed for three months. I knew that after my last job I wanted to stay in stereotypical "women's issues." I felt passionate about every organization I interviewed with, but really connected with A Safe Place, a local domestic violence agency. Without sharing too much (very unlike me), this is the one area of my life that I seldom, if ever, discuss. Most people do not know that I was a victim of violence and abuse in college during a nearly two-year relationship. Even I had put it out of my mind as the years passed. But now, here it was staring me in the face again.

My husband, ever supportive, was worried that working there might bring up too many things that I had already worked through. But I felt strong enough to proceed. I knew it was vitally important work. Raising money for this organization was literally saving lives every single day.

While A Safe Place predominantly serves women and their children, the structure and tone of the agency didn't feel "feminine" to me.

I'm not sure why that was. It was led by a fascinating, passionate and smart woman with a predominantly female staff - warm, supportive and driven. Maybe it was because it was structured more like a for-profit business than the other agencies where I had worked. Regardless, I felt proud and truly valued as part of the executive team.

Finally, after many years, I was back up to the salary I had turned down at the logistics company! It only took 15 years. I had fabulous team members reporting to me: smart, eager, passionate - everything I could possibly want! It was extremely hard work, but unimaginably fulfilling. Everywhere I looked, we were making a real difference in the lives of people that I actually saw - children, too. It was important work. Heartwork as it's called. I have no words for what I received working here.

Knock. Knock. Who's there? Life.

For the second time in my life, and after only one short year, I was laid off. The agency was taking a bold new direction to utilize contractors and consultants for their fundraising and development work to leverage specialties and expertise. I knew what the books looked like, so I can't say I was completely surprised. But it did take a toll on my self-esteem.

Close my eyes and jump

Surprisingly, being laid off this time was actually the impetus for me finally striking out on my own. This was an opportunity! They offered me a chance to continue working with them on a contractual basis. Was I interested? Hmm. Could I really start my own consulting and coaching business?

Wow! What an interesting idea – my own business! Can I do it? Do I *want* to do it? Should I do it? Well, here's what happened next. After a very short conversation with my husband, and with his unconditional support, I decided to do it. No drawn out thinking or planning. I wasn't following any long-held dream, just my "gut." So, taking advantage of what was laid out in front of me, I closed my eyes and jumped!

Now that I was committed - heck, I already had my first client - I knew I had to sit down and actually make a plan. Seriously, this was a real struggle for me. I don't plan. I fly by the seat of my pants. I take things as they come. But at least for this part of my business, planning was non-negotiable.

Lucky for me, I was once again surrounded by incredible people who supported me. First and foremost, is my husband and biggest fan, Rich. He constantly tells me that I can do this and that he'll support me no matter what. Even as I continue to refine my business, his support never wavers. And believe me, I can test this man!

Once I committed to start my own consulting firm, I looked at the rest of my support system and network. I had a lot of connections, but it had been quite a while since I had connected. I started doing what I should have done years ago; I reached out, re-connected and re-strengthened those relationships. Life happens. People get busy and circumstances change. I know this. Still the vast majority of people were happy to re-connect, and this was a great excuse.

One of those relationships (we never really did lose touch), was an amazing woman I first met more than 15 years ago through RESOLVE. She had her own wonderfully successful business, so I knew she could help me out, or at least commiserate! Lucky for me, she not only offered up her support and expertise, she introduced me to other amazing women. In fact, they are the amazing co-authors of this book! Paula keeps me on my toes and holds me accountable. She balances me out. She is as steady and organized as I am a free spirit. Honestly, I cannot imagine how this would have happened without her. Love!

Happily un-planned

As I turn 50, I have new ways to describe myself. I'm a business owner, consultant, life coach, speaker, and now author. And I absolutely love it! I feel passionate about what I'm doing. It feels like "me." My work is personal. I don't have the energy or desire to hide from my experiences. Passion is leading me. I just know that it feels "right."

I'm still exploring and learning each day. With the support of my family and friends, including the guidance of some incredible, fabulous and strong women, I keep moving forward. So many people share themselves generously if I ask. They offer advice, encouragement, and a good kick in the pants – whatever I need. (Side note: It seems most of the women I'm drawn to have also experienced their own infertility…a theme in my life that I've come to embrace.)

This is a personal growing process. I know this. But I have options. I know this too.

And one more thing I know for sure – this is where I'm supposed to be…even though I never planned it.

Get to Know Kari Skloot

After more than 25 years working with organizations of all shapes and sizes, for-profit and non-profit, Kari followed her own path and founded Skloot Consulting, LLC. As a certified life coach, consultant, public speaker and author, Kari started the business to work with non-profit organizations in areas of capacity building and resource development. Recently she added the Life-Work Coach division to focus on helping women flip their thinking about balance. ***Put Your LIFE First!*** This unique spin on the traditional question of balance encourages all women to keep life and work in perspective and to define their own personal balance and success. She provides individual coaching, group and specialized executive director coaching, and speaks on a myriad of topics.

Kari and her fabulous husband of over 26 years, Rich, live in the northwest suburbs of Chicago with their brilliant and extremely athletic 15-year-old son, sweet pit-bull mix, and the crazy cat that lets them all live in the house!

Connect with Kari:
    847-778-8219
    Kari@sklootconsulting.com
    Life-Work-Coach.com
    Facebook.com/TheLifeWorkCoach Twitter.com/Life_Work_Coach

Kari has named the non-profit organizations she has worked for in the hope that readers who need support for themselves or their loved ones will reach out for information or services. Additionally, she encourages others to research, explore and support these wonderful agencies.

RESOLVE: The National Infertility Association
www.resolve.org

American Cancer Society
www.cancer.org

Women's Health Foundation
www.womenshealthfoundation.org

A Safe Place
www.asafeplaceforhelp.org

A Kick in the Pants

By Ashlee Niethammer, Women/Girls Clothing Designer

As I sit here getting set to embark on the story of my company's origins, I have to ask myself a few questions. First, what in the world am I thinking? And secondly, can I truly put into words all that has gone into creating such a huge, meaningful part of my life?

Without a doubt, my company is a reflection of me. It has its successes, big and small, its failures, its ups, downs and in-betweens. Above all, it is tangible and real, and a reflection of the artist within me. I will be forever grateful and humbled to be able to show that to the world.

Despite my apprehensions about putting pen to paper, I want to present to you, to myself and especially to my two young, impressionable daughters, how my own line of apparel got its start.

Right here, in black and white, is the story of my life. I can only hope someone can learn from it and that as I write, I too can continue learning and growing. I also hope to uncover the true path of how this all came about, and invite you as the reader to come on the journey with me.

Let me first start by defining my business. It is a small apparel company that designs and sells women's and girl's clothing. The best part is its name – *oakie&b* – the loving nicknames of my two beautiful little girls, Oakleigh and Brix. My brand name is *oakie&b kicky&cool apparel*. My husband Mike wanted oak&b, but it sounded a bit too masculine for a girl's brand. Maybe one day a men's/boy's brand can be an offshoot named oak&b. Who knows, right? Anything is possible if you want it to be.

What does kicky mean? It truly is a word. I'd never heard it before; it means exciting or fashionable. It really defines what I envisioned for the brand.

Filling a niche

What sparked the creation of my company was a clear desire to fill a space, or a niche, that I firmly believed was missing or lacking for women and for children. As a mother of two little girls, constantly on the run, wearing the many hats of a homemaker, I wanted to look cute but also feel good doing it. Tight jeans were out, as were dresses; and sweatpants were not flattering enough. I was left with cute workout gear. Again, there was this "space" that wasn't filled - cute, easy-to-wear clothing that was both comfy and funky. If it could transition into evening or a quick happy hour with friends, then it would be even better!

Did those clothes exist? Certainly, not the kind I like. I wanted to create clothing for children that filled that same niche too. I wanted something edgy, artistic and effortlessly hip to wear to do all my running around in; and I wanted my kiddos to have the same vibe.

My girls are growing and don't always agree with my vibe, but I constantly work on letting them create their own look expressing themselves through clothing. That is essentially how I got my own start.

As I reflect on my younger years, my path to the clothing business seemed to take time to reveal itself. Truth be told, it revealed itself several times in my life, but I chose to ignore it. I do believe throughout your life you are given clues. You just need to unravel them. If you're not paying attention, they just whiz by. I actually saw these clues and can remember a lot of them, but I thought I would be better off doing something that would make me more money in the long run. The reality is I would probably be making more money now if I had chosen to take those early clues and go for it.

But you cannot live in the past. You need to move forward and go for it. Try out your passions and you could really surprise yourself. I am a perfect example of that. If someone told me this is what I'd be doing right now, I wouldn't have believed it. I am not some huge million dollar company (maybe someday), but guess what? It is mine. My girl's names are the brand; and I am writing this now to tell you about it. That in itself is pretty cool!

The inspiration

Where does inspiration come from? For me, it took many forms. I am always wide-eyed and observant. I consider myself a very visual learner and also extremely open -- open to possibilities, and to trying out things that others usually don't or won't.

I have never been afraid of being different in fashion. I've always liked to stand out with what I choose to wear. In fact, I often wonder if I hide behind the clothes I wear? Let me explain. I have a chronic skin disease called Vitiligo. It's what Michael Jackson had. You lose pigment in your skin and end up with white patches all over. Mine changes and is not as bad as some have it. I had a friend call me "a human lava lamp" once, and he wasn't too far off. By having this on my skin, I was forced to find ways to camouflage the Vitiligo. I would wear things that hid it from people, or mostly from me.

There are times that the Vitiligo is hard on me mentally. But with age and motherhood, I've come to better terms with all of it. I don't want my girls to hide from what they are or their imperfections. As a result, I grow a little each year and don't hide behind the clothes as much. I love that song by Pink, "Perfect Imperfections." We all have something we believe is not perfect about ourselves, and we have to find ways to believe they are perfect to us. Like most things in life, it is about perspective.

The reason for this explanation is that, I believe the Vitiligo was, in fact, my first inspiration. It motivated me to get creative with my fashion. Maybe the Vitiligo was one of those early clues of what I would do later in life. It was given to me to learn something, to push me to get creative.

At age seven or eight, I remember having this jean shirt with my name on the back in iron-on, flowered letters. I grew out of it, but I loved it. So I tried to pull the letters off and fix it to say "Shea" instead of "Ashlee." Shea is my little brother. I tried to turn that shirt I loved into a shirt for him. He was little, so a little jean shirt with flowered letters would not be so bad. This is super funny to me now because my little brother is pretty much a man's man. I'm not sure I ever told him about this or the other times I tried to dress him up in girlie clothes, but there must be pictures out there somewhere.

Another source of my inspiration stemmed from my dear friend Raena's mother, Lisa. Our moms were friends since we were very young. Since they were both single moms, we all lived together at one point to save money. I know what you're thinking. No they were not a couple. Raena's mother Lisa was, in my opinion, one cool chic. She was an early inspiration to me for fashion. In fact, she oozed fashion coolness. She was a hair dresser and edgy in a very classy way. She also had a rockin' body, so she could wear some pretty sexy things. I would just look at her and think, "Wow!" I eventually got old enough to fit in some of her things. I never filled them out the way she did, but I sure tried.

Lisa and Raena moved just outside San Francisco because Lisa got very ill and needed better care. I visited several times. San Francisco became another inspiration along with my visits to see them. Lisa's taste in clothes got more extravagant living there, and I got more mesmerized by what she wore. Not to mention, I was visiting a very cool city - a city that had so much going on, and people who dressed so much differently from where I was living at the time. Raena would take me to Haight/Ashbury area where I felt excited about everything I saw: the clothes, the people, the energy. I felt alive and inspired.

Lisa left us way too early. Her sickness took her life. I know if she were here today she would still be inspiring me with her awesome fashion sense. As I am writing this now I feel like she is smiling at me. I know she would be happy to know the impact she had on me growing up and coming into my own fashion.

My mother was, and continues to be, a source of inspiration for me. Although not as edgy as Lisa, she is always put together. She has a great way of combining colors, fabrics and accessories. I am sure that watching her get dressed for work and many other occasions all my life taught me a thing or two about fashion. Even now we show up in outfits that are similar, or pick the same color scheme. She didn't always agree with what I put together, but my mom always let me be me. That is a gift in itself. I never remember a time I had to fit into some kind of mold she had for me. I was me growing up, not who or what others wanted me to be.

I didn't grow up with much money or have a lot, but I learned how to mix outfits up and pair them with different accessories to make each outfit seem different. I was really into clothes at an early age, and without much money, I worked pretty young. I had jobs at TJ Maxx and a store called Sagebrush, both clothing stores. I was maybe fourteen or fifteen working hard to earn those clothes I wanted so badly. I was even nominated for best dressed my senior year. I know its nuts that I remember that; but I guess because I worked so hard for those clothes it stuck with me. That nomination meant something to me.

My husband Mike thinks it's weird that I remember that and I may have even saved the paper that states that fact. I will have to look for that memorabilia to show to my girls and make my husband cringe. By the way my husband has known me since I was eleven. So, we graduated together. I bet he remembers what he was nominated for our senior year. He just won't admit to it.

Being able to travel and live in different cities such as San Francisco, LA, Chicago, New York and Denver fueled my passion for all things fashion. I am totally obsessed with fashion magazines, fashion shows and real live street fashion (which is completely the best kind to me). Living and visiting some of these fashion-centered cities filled me with energy. In fact, there is nothing better than watching street fashion in NYC. If you look in any city, really, you can find great people watching. Now if you get a chance to do people/fashion watching in other countries, that's where it gets really cool and exciting. Seeing what is hip and fashion forward in other countries is truly amazing. I have been lucky enough to have visited many other countries in my life thus far. Some people travel for the sights, but I admit I travel for fashion, and maybe a little of the sights too.

The long and winding career path

My career path to entrepreneur began in some rather unsuspecting places. The short version is I graduated college with a Wellness and Preventative Medicine degree. To this day I am still fascinated with medicine, exercise and the human body, so it was not a total waste.

At one point I questioned my degree and switched to the Fashion Merchandising degree. I was trying to listen to those inner clues. As I stated before, I thought I would never make money at it, so I switched back.

I spent several years using my degree. I even sold surgical equipment at one point, which I soon realized was not for me. I was gaining valuable sales skills and the money was there, but my heart was not in it. I even remember feeling out of my own body. Now if that's not a clue, then I don't know what is! One of my favorite quotes comes from Karen Moning, "The most confused we ever get is when we try to convince our heads of something we know is a lie."

At last, I began to follow my heart and my passion. I left the money and the stress and basically started over. I worked for ESPRIT. (Remember that clothing company?) I was a Visual Merchandiser for them, making half of what I was making as a sales rep for medical equipment. I sucked it up. Unfortunately, ESPRIT was bought out and I lost my job. Still, I gained invaluable sales experience with them. Next up was a job with Skechers running the Chicago Showroom. This was awesome for me. I was traveling, working with the latest in shoe fashion, and really getting a taste of the industry.

Soon after, my husband and I were married. His job took us to NYC for an eighteen month stint. YES! YES! YES! Skechers had no position for me there, sadly. The upside was I would be moving to the fashion capitol of the U.S. I spent some time going back to school while I was there. NYC living teaches you a thing or two about fashion. Street fashion there is like no other. Each area of New York has its own sense of style. It was so fun to discover that and create a fashion mixture of it all.

After the eighteen months were up, we were ready to start a family. We moved to Colorado where our two little girls were born, and I became a full-time mom. I say full-time because our girls are twenty months apart, and it was pretty busy early on. Oh, who am I kidding? It's still busy now. I have these two amazing little ones, running them around here and there, to classes, sports lessons and friends' houses. What to wear to all this?

Love those pants!

I told you about all the things that were not going to work for me. So let's talk about the things that did. I had a cool ass pair of pants I picked up in NYC. They were in that not-sweat-pant, not-tight-pant, not-workout-pant space, but cute and flexible. The problem was that they were only in a summer fabric and I wore them out! The other problem was they were super loose. I was getting my figure back from the two kids and wanted something a little more streamlined. So, I thought if I wanted some cool funky pants to wear all the time, other moms would too.

Well, lucky for me my amazing mother-in-law, Lois, can sew. She can also make patterns. So we got out the worn-out pants and recreate them. Streamlined, reshaped, twisted and boom, the pant I wanted was born. I picked jersey and gauze fabric for the sample. I absolutely loved them, and wondered if we could duplicate them for my daughters. So we created them in their sizes. Whenever my girls and I wore the pants, strangers would flock to us demanding to know where we found them. My friends asked if my mother-in-law could make them a pair. As I farmed out my mother-in-law to altruistically recreate these pants for all my friends, it dawned on me that I may just have found my Ah-ha moment! Ok- so it knocked me over the head in a not-so-subtle way. The point is, this time I listened.

I will never forget being literally stalked by people at Target with my girls and my mom wearing our pants. I mean people were seriously following us and peering around corners! I feel like a kid when I say this, but really, you can go ask my mom. I think even she was like, 'Whoa, what is going on here?' It was then I knew I had something. I wasn't sure how to begin, but I had something. I had something people wanted. Great - a good idea, but ….

Sew now what?

Embarking on this project would prove challenging because I do not sew, nor have I ever learned. I never made a pattern and had never really stepped foot into a fabric store. These things had to be figured out. Oh, and what will we call these little gems? As I mentioned before, we called them oakie&b after my girls' nicknames. I played with fonts, wrote it out and oakie&b kicky&cool apparel was born. This all seems fast, but that's because it was. Once I made the decision to actually start the process, that's what I did. I went for it.

So I had a name. Now I needed to get a pattern made, pick out fabric, find a seamstress, get a label made, put it all together and go out and sell these pants. And I was confident that these pants would sell. How do you do all this without a shred of experience? The answer- Google after Google, it's all about networking. For the most part I have found people to be very open and forthcoming about advice and information. I searched and found a local seamstress, designed a label online, had my mother in law make the first pattern, and went to the fabric store to see what I liked.

Then I dropped off the fabric, the labels and the pattern to a seamstress. Out came some oakie&b pants. I did a small run of pants, maybe thirty between kids and women's, and I sold them all in just two weeks! Once sold I would wait for feedback to see what should be improved. Since most were sold to friends and their kids, I received the feedback needed to move to the next phase

And then it began to spread.

I made enough money to buy more for the next round, tweaked the pattern in response to feedback, and off I was again to make some more. I then sold *those* in just two weeks. I literally was selling these pants left and right, mostly to friends and their kids but, whatever, they were selling.

So I continued, and things were going well. I was surprised how well it was going. But I was not making money. My seamstress was too expensive. I was buying retail fabric, and I was mostly selling to friends (at a discounted price). I don't want to make all of this sound super easy, because there were many challenges, but I knew I had something that was a sure thing. I felt positive that this was a pant every mom and girl would want and need. It filled that space for funky, functional fashion.

I researched more to find someone that could sew them faster and for less. I found wholesale fabric that I could buy, and away I went. I even got a Groupon for a photo-shoot. The girls and I went to this little photography studio where they shot the best pictures of me and the girls in these pants. These pictures mean so much to me. Nothing has really compared since. Maybe it's because it was the start. Those pictures are proof of a small little company - my small company - being born.

Did you say Cleveland?

With everything taking off, my contacts established, and a business in its fragile infancy years, my husband took a job in Cleveland. Cleveland?! By the time we moved, I had about 1,000 pairs of oakie&b pants, both kids and women's. I didn't know a soul in Cleveland. Who was going to buy these pants? Where would I even start? I would soon find out.

We moved in August, so at least it wasn't the dead of winter. During winter in Chagrin Falls, you basically have to hibernate because it's cold and it snows a ton. It was nice and warm upon our arrival. Immediately after getting somewhat settled into our new house, I began trying to figure out how to get my inventory sold. I decide to dress my daughters and myself in the pants and walk through our cute little village where people were out shopping, eating, and walking. Chagrin Falls is somewhat of a tourist attraction, a lucky happenstance for me. Like before, people began stopping us inquiring about the pants. I started handing out cards and noticed people pointing at our pants. At this point I felt pretty good inside, even confident that these pants were going to translate to this area as they did in Denver-testimony to the fact that people everywhere love new and interesting things.

The following week I was signing my preschooler up for her class and noticed a cool yoga studio next door. I decided to check it out. Yes, of course I was wearing my oakie&b pants. I walked in and the gal at the front desk went crazy over my pants. She took a photo of them and sent it to the owner. And she immediately wanted my pants for the front store. Wow, just like that she placed an order. But as she did, I realized I had never sold wholesale before; this was an entirely new arena. Again, I Googled how to do an invoice, pulled the pants for the store, dropped it all off and boom! Just like that, pants began selling like crazy. I soon realized it was pretty cool to have my clothes in stores. So I ventured into the children's store here in town, and they too began to carry my pants.

I have to say the one thing that makes oakie&b successful is that I truly believe in my product. Once you wear my pants or have your kiddo wear them, you will love them too. I cannot tell you how many people tell me the same story. It is always about how they were wearing my clothes and getting stopped left and right; how they felt so cool because of all the compliments they got. Others said their kid was in the pants and people were writing down where to get them. It's these stories that propel me forward and keep me going.

I am sometimes referred to as the "Pant Lady" in town. It's so funny to meet someone new and they ask what I do. Once I tell them, nine out of ten times they say, "Oh yeah, you're that pant lady." I have to say it is so exciting for me to walk into Starbucks and see someone in line ahead wearing my clothes. I often help out at my daughter's school and there are always a few kids roaming the halls or in the lunch room in my clothes. That is so rewarding.

Maybe you have heard of Zulily, a website where you can get discounted clothes by all kinds of designers. I sent them my website address as an introduction to my clothing. They said they would host a sale for me. It's a national website so this was big stuff. My first sale I sold out. That told me that it wasn't just a small town thing. I have done several since. I also partake in many holiday-type shows for exposure. Sometimes the shows are for profit, other times they are marketing- both are necessary.

So much for days off

With any business it's sometimes hard to keep going. There are days I wonder if I should. Why? Well, it's our job to second guess ourselves, isn't it? But just as I start to lose steam, some new opportunity presents itself. These are the clues in life that you have to pay attention to. I started this little business on a belief that my clothes were something people would really want. I wanted my own thing and I wanted to also show my two girls that if you believe, you can achieve. I am very lucky in so many ways. I had so much support around me to start this business. I have the love and support of my husband who handed me a check for ten thousand dollars and a business plan he had done for me, because he believed in me. I have the support of my mother-in-law who always tries so hard to help me in any way I need.

My mother has been an advocate from the beginning. She has not only given me the confidence boost we all need once in a while, but has helped with shows and tagging and bagging and all that comes with this business. Likewise, my friends have been incredibly encouraging. And last, but not least, my girls Oakleigh and Brix deserve the most credit. They allow me to take precious moments from them at times for the business. They even help me count and fold, and most of all, sell the clothes by wearing them.

I had a few friends write something to put in here so you didn't just have to hear me the whole time. Below are the quotes from them.

Sue Reid (daughters 10 and 6)

"Wearing oakie&b is not only about the reaction I get from people, the wow factor, the questions "Where did you get those?" and "how can I order them?" More importantly it is about the feeling I get deep inside when wearing the clothing. It is this overwhelming confidence, this special feeling that can't be described. Bottom line, in oakie&b, I feel like a rock star. I love learning how to couple an oakie&b piece with my regular, everyday clothes. I've transformed long tops into dresses for work, made complete with a high boot or heel; or I've thrown on a white T and a jean jacket with a pair of oakie&b pants. The possibilities are endless, and the result is nothing short of awesome."

Christy Rosneck

"oakie&b apparel is everything the brand advertises, kicky, cool and fun! Ashlee's designs perfectly deliver clothing that is both stylish and comfortable. The pants and tunics can be worn around the house or dressed up for an afternoon of errands or drinks in the evening with friends. Every time I wear oakie&b I am literally stopped in my tracks! People really respond to the funky prints and innovative design. My eight year old daughter loves the clothing as well. We can't help but feel amazing when sporting the oakie&b apparel.

Truly the best part for my daughter and me is how amazing Ashlee and her daughters are as people and friends. Knowing the woman behind the brand makes wearing the clothing special. Ashlee has many talents and gifts, but her kind and gracious heart is her greatest asset."

♪♪♪

I'm here to tell you that if you pay attention to yourself, and really listen, the right things will happen. You too can start a business if that is your desire. I now not only do pants, but have expanded into tops, tunics, leggings, wraptops and headbands. The business moves and grows at its own pace, but I did it. Sometimes you can surprise yourself if you just put your energy into the right thing. Follow your passion. That sounds like it should be easy. I know it's not easy. Look how long it took me to figure it out. But it is all possible.

It's all posssible; and the best part is what you learn during the process. I will leave you with one last message, a quote from Fabienne Fredrickson. It reads, "The things you are passionate about are not random, they are your calling."

About Ashlee

Ashlee Niethammer is owner and designer of oakie&b kicky&cool apparel. She lives in Chagrin Falls, OH with her two daughters Oakleigh (aka oakie), Brix (aka b) and husband Mike.

Website: www.oakieandb.com
E-mail: oakieandb@yahoo.com
facebook: oakieandb

Do What You Love

By Dorothy Deemer, Massage Therapist

I liked my job, I really did. I was a computer programmer, using COBOL on a PC. COBOL is an acronym for "Common Business Oriented Language". It was usually used only on Mainframe computers. This was in the late 80s and early 90s. I was very proud to be working at this company, because everyone that worked there was VERY smart.

Before I started this job, I did two rounds at College. The first time earned a BA in Economics and Business; but more importantly, I made life-long friends and had a great time. These same friends organized, decorated, and executed my late-in-life wedding. The second time I actually did my studying, earned really good grades and a BS in Computer Information Systems. As a result, I started my real career five years later than most of my peers.

Hence, my manager was a few years younger than me. Not that this was a problem; but because of his youth, he wasn't very experienced. At my annual review, all he really had to say was "you wander away from your desk too much." I was shocked. He said nothing about how I was getting projects done in a timely manner, and nothing about how the code I wrote was error-free. Also, nothing about how my positive attitude and sunny disposition contributed to an excellent work environment. Just the wandering.

Now (with wisdom from age), I understand his issue was that he thought, in my "wandering," I was probably disrupting other people's work. But at the time, I concluded (correctly) that a 'desk job' was not the best place for me. I needed work that required movement, not work that required sitting still.

Let the soul-searching begin!

I was very fortunate that at the time I had a great friend at the office, who also didn't feel suited to the job she had. Together we brainstormed to discover our work place in the world. Lots of reading of good books and lots of conversations later, she went to nursing school; I went to massage school.

Giving a massage requires that I move! And giving a massage helps people. While the real push to change my career was so that I was moving my body as part of my work, I also wasn't thrilled with what I was doing at my corporate job - creating reports for people working at other companies.

Every Saturday from 9am to 3pm, and every Tuesday and Thursday evening from 7pm to 9:30pm, I drove into Chicago for classes. It was a huge time commitment, and a solid one hour commute in each direction, but was TONS of fun! I enjoyed learning about muscles, bones, and the human body. As a bonus, I was receiving some bodywork every week. Even a massage from a learner is better than no massage at all! The program was a full year from beginning to end. I graduated in August of 1993.

During the course of that year of learning, things changed, as they always do in a year. My job changed slightly and got more interesting. So I wasn't itching to embark on a career as a Massage Therapist. In fact, I was terrified to make a change and way too comfortable at my secure corporate job to consider quitting. How could I quit a well-paid job at a company that made contributions to my 401K even when I didn't, provided great benefits (including a free lunch), and plenty of vacation time? So I didn't quit, and I (only occasionally) gave massages. I was enjoying my corporate job. I was on a team of smart, fun people, and felt like I was making a contribution. The team was very collaborative, and we all enjoyed solving issues together. These were the golden years of my career.

Fast forward several years to the fall of 1999. I got a massage at the health club where I was a member - the WORST massage I have ever received. Seriously, she smeared some massage oil on me and didn't address any muscles. After the massage was over, I went to the front desk to pay; the Massage Therapist was already gone. The woman at the desk asked, "How great that you just received a massage. How was it?"

I didn't want to lie, so I said, "Well, I'm a tough critic because I'm a Massage Therapist, but it wasn't very good." The only thing she heard was, "I'm a Massage Therapist."

"You're a Massage Therapist?" she asked. "Do you want a job?" She quickly turned to the woman standing behind her, and said, "Pam, she's a Massage Therapist!" And Pam came round the desk to stand right beside me, and asked, "Do you want a job?"

"No!" I said, and thought to myself, I have a job.

But Pam was persistent, "Really, just every other Saturday afternoon." What's a person to do when a job falls into her lap? I took the job, and I LOVED it! And I got paid doing something I loved.

3

Meanwhile, back at my real job... A few years earlier I had moved into the role of manager of other programmers. I didn't feel like I was very good at it. I had only half the skills needed to be really good.

Though I was a great encourager and helper to my team members, I wasn't good as a mentor. I didn't know how to find opportunities for my staff and push them to grow and advance.

I now know that networking with other managers at the company was how I would have found these opportunities; but I didn't know what networking was, or how to do that then.

At this company, they had something called "working managers." I had projects just like my staff, and was also supposed to be a manager. I felt like I was barely keeping my head above water, and didn't feel I had the time and energy to do more for my staff. As it is on any team, I had people that I should have been pushing up, and others who needed coaching to do their jobs properly. The fires (people who were not performing well) got any extra attention that I had. And THAT was not fun work for me. I didn't have the time or energy to look for the opportunities to push the great performers in a new direction.

Feeling unsettled, I was dreaming and reading about taking time off from my job. The book I read was *Six Months off: How to Plan, Negotiate, & Take the Break You Need Without Burning Bridges or Going Broke* by Hope Dlugozima, James Scott, & David Sharp. Sort of like a college professor taking a sabbatical, but without the research requirement. As luck would have it, our team was a little over-staffed, and my manager was more than happy to get me off the payroll for the summer of 2000. My last day of work that spring was the Friday before Memorial Day weekend, and I went back to work the Monday after Labor Day, for a total of 15 weeks!

One of the many discoveries or insights that resulted from being off work was how much I didn't miss it! Sleeping as much as I wanted, no alarm to wake me, and doing whatever I wanted every day was wonderful. The first part of my time I spent at the library reading whatever caught my attention.

I was 39 years old that summer, didn't have a husband, much less a boyfriend that could become a husband, and all I'd ever wanted to do was become a mommy. But being a mommy without a husband was NOT an option for me. So I needed to let go of that dream and hope.

Books about making a life without having children jumped off the shelves at the library for me. I was very grateful that I had that time to get my mind around a different life plan.

Besides altering my life goal, I always dreamed of taking a long bike ride. In the *Six Months off* book there were some ideas for things to do while off work. One of them was going on an organized bike ride. The booked mentioned a group called Wandering Wheels that planned an around-the-country ride that summer. They started in San Francisco in March, rode to Los Angeles, then across the USA to Georgia. From Georgia, the group rode to New York City, and across the USA again to Seattle. I joined them there and we rode to San Francisco. It was a 3 week ride, with 2 days off for a total of 1056 miles. It was the MOST difficult physical event I had ever done. Not only was it physically challenging, but I experienced emotional growth as well.

Before going on the trip I had established some expectations in my mind that I didn't even realize I had. When the trip wasn't what I expected, the disappointment was crushing. In the literature that I read before the trip, there was talk about music and fun around the campfire, and the development of a community. Well, most of the people on the trip had been riding together since March. They were DONE with campfires and community. Also, they were all very strong riders and I was not. I felt like I was riding my bike as fast as possible and always the last one to camp each night. They had no interest in, and I had no energy for, singing around the campfire. But I'm still proud of that accomplishment, and glad I can cross it off my bucket list.

4

September 11th, 2000 (not THE September 11th; that was the next year), I went back to work - UGH! After a few weeks, or months (I don't actually remember), my manager and I had a conversation. I knew that managing other people was not really what I wanted to do. Apparently, I was not the only person at my level of experience and seniority who didn't want to manage people, but whose pay rate was too high to step back from managing. My manager, and probably some others at his management level, came up with a new role for me and others like me. It sounded fine (I almost wrote 'great', but really 'fine' is a more accurate word), and I took it.

I won't even try to give you all the boring details of the work; but I will just say that after six months I was not thriving, and I was scared. I was moved to a new manager; again he was several years younger than me. Essentially I was demoted, although not in my pay, thankfully. I was no longer the shining star that my prior manager thought I was. This was NOT a fun place to be, and I felt confused. I didn't know what to do.

In January 2002, I decided I needed to quit and really give a massage practice a try. In the years since graduating from Massage School, I met and became good friends with someone who was making his living as a Massage Therapist. He was open about how much money he made and how he built his business. With his encouragement, I spent several months getting my brain around making this big of a change. I got serious about putting every dime I could find into savings and starting to build a client base. I finally quit my corporate job on May 31, 2002.

5

I didn't have a business plan. I don't think I'd ever even heard of that. But I did have my own ideas of what I would do. I figured if I couldn't make enough money to pay my mortgage and bills, I could sell my house and move to Iowa City. Why Iowa City you might ask? I went to College (the first time) in Iowa, and I have a great friend that lives there. I knew that the cost of living was a little more reasonable there, compared to the Chicago-land area where I lived. I could buy a house (paid in full) with the proceeds from my current home. Not having a mortgage to pay, I could build a massage practice there.

If things were really dire and the Iowa City option wouldn't work, I could stay in Illinois, sell my house, and move in with my mom. Those two plans were all I had for a "business plan". I had no idea how to do marketing, and as it turned out, I didn't have to. My clients marketed for me. My business was built on referrals alone.

During this time, I continued to work at the health club giving massages. Having a place to work out for free was a huge plus to working there, and sometimes people I met would want to get a massage in their home. That was a great source of clients.

Around 2005, I had the opportunity to be the manager of the massage team at the health club. What?!?! Ok, so we all know that I really didn't like being a manager in the corporate setting. It was years later and a completely different atmosphere. Managing a team of massage therapists was an opportunity to see if I would like to one day build my private practice to the point of hiring other therapists. I really enjoyed managing the financials and scheduling. Managing the other Massage Therapists should have been no problem.

Honestly, what is there to manage? Did they arrive to their appointment in a timely manner? Are there any complaints about the massage? Seems like a no brainer. But I never expected that the people who had been my colleagues and friends would become so adversarial, just because I was the "manager." It was a bizarre experience to say the least. In just 6 months, I was able to re-remember that I don't really like managing people.

Fortunately, about the time I'd decided I didn't want to be the manager anymore, the upper management decided to re-consolidate the management roles. I was back to being just another massage therapist, and my friends became my friends again. I had learned a lot about people and about myself. The most important lesson being that what I really wanted to do was give massages.

The marketing plan of relying heavily on referrals, worked great through 2007, which was my best financial year. With the Market Crash in 2008, things changed. Some of my clients lost their jobs, and some had to move to a different state for a new job. Finding new clients wasn't as easy as it had been in 2002.

In those few years from 2002 to 2010 or so, people started to use the internet much more to find services such as massage. Also, national massage chains started to pop up in every town. I didn't have a website and I wasn't listed in the Yellow Pages. Massage ads in the phone book are separated into "Therapeutic" and "Non-Therapeutic". I would certainly be listed under "Therapeutic", but I just didn't like the idea of being listed near the Massage ad that starts with *"5'7" to 5'11" - Petite or Curvy"* or *"24 hours - Honey Massage."* My massage practice was in my home, and I didn't want strangers calling, and coming in for a massage. I didn't want to worry about what "type" of massage they were looking for either!

By 2010, I decided to join a networking organization and actually do some marketing. The group was made up of entrepreneurs that help each other find new business. Knowing a new group of people helped me expand my client base. Then in 2012, in this same group, I met my husband (a nice side benefit of networking that I NEVER expected) and moved my practice from my home into an office.

My office had been in my home since I started my practice, but the logistics of fitting my husband, myself, and my clients into a shared space didn't work. I'd always wondered what it would be like to run my business out of an office instead of my home; and now I got to see how that would work. Along with an office, I created a business name - Kneading Works Massage Therapy - and a website. My website is linked to online appointment scheduling, but I'm still not in the phone book; it is just too creepy.

Working away from home has its pluses and its minuses. In an office, I am much more comfortable allowing strangers to make an appointment. I can advertise more easily. When I had my business in my home, the massage room was not AT ALL separate from my living area. It was the second bedroom on the 2nd floor. The office/desk area was my dining room table. However, it was great for me to be at home until a client arrived and not have any commute time. I could easily have a meal between clients or just before someone arrived. And I could get the sheets into the laundry between clients. I don't have laundry facilities at my office, so I have to take all the sheets for the day home to be washed and ready to go back to the office the next morning.

Would I do it all over again? YES!! Do I sometimes wonder what my life would be like had I stayed the course in the corporate world? Yes, sometimes, but mostly I'm very grateful that I took a hard left turn and am on a totally different path. Truthfully, I was making more money annually in 2002 when I left my corporate job, than I ever have doing my massage business. But in many ways I'm more secure out on my own. I can't really get laid-off, and I'm SURE I would have been let go from that corporation.

There's a saying that is, "do what you love, and the money will come." I think it is more accurate to say, "Do what you love, and the money doesn't matter." Of course, you need to make enough money to eat and have shelter, but if you don't need to escape from your life (read "job"), or need lots of extra money to go on vacations and buy things, it isn't as important.

My next dream is to have my practice back in my home, but with a separate entrance for my clients that I can access from the inside. Until then, you can find me through my website: www.KneadingWorks.com. Call me to make an appointment or ask more about my journey. 847-602-0793. My name is Dorothy Deemer.

Dorothy Deemer
Owner, Massage Therapist
Kneading Works Massage Therapy
Dorothy@KneadingWorks.com
www.KneadingWorks.com
P: 847.602.0793
Feel good, be well.

How I Found My Voice, and Became Theirs

By Pam Labellarte, Special Education Advocate

Change is neither good nor bad; it's necessary for growth. Change is also one of the underlying themes of my life. I was born the oldest of five children in the 1950's, in a family where both parents worked full time outside of the home. Most of my friends came home after school and played outside until they were called home for dinner. On the contrary, at the young age of nine, I arrived home from school and faced a myriad of responsibilities, including caring for my younger siblings, doing odd chores around the house and getting dinner started. This seemed so unfair to me at the time. But once I was an adult and on my own, I soon found this was a gift. More about that later.

Because my father was in construction, we moved a great deal. By the time I left home at 18, I had lived in 11 different houses in 3 states and attended 8 different schools. Because I was always "the new kid," I quickly developed skills to adapt to different situations and people - skills I would hone and utilize on my life's journey.

My father's dream

My father left school after 8th grade to work on the farm and then joined the Army during WWII. His dream was for me to graduate from college. But his early death at the age of 52 changed everything.

Though I was only 17 and a senior in high school, I assumed the role of "the other parent" to my four siblings, ages 15, 10, 7 and 5. The challenges of my new role made me more determined to do everything in my power to attend college and fulfill my father's dream. My hard work paid off and I earned a tuition free scholarship to a Carthage College, a private school within commuting distance of my home. I needed to commute because I couldn't afford the cost of campus housing, and I had a job to help support my siblings.

Since my early childhood I was challenged with hyperactivity and a severe case of procrastination. The extra energy allowed me to pull off miracles like meeting project deadlines at the last minute and successfully cramming for exams the night before finals. These bad habits would soon be my demise. As I faced the demands of a full case load of college class work, a 30 hour a week job, and the responsibilities of being the "other parent," I soon realized that my father's dream was out of my reach. At the time I was dealing with "invisible" challenges that wouldn't be uncovered until almost thirty years later.

Women don't fit in with truck drivers and warehouse people

After dropping out of college I left home, and spent the next nine years under the guidance of a select group of mentors. Starting at an entry level position with the Distribution Department of an international medical supplier, I developed a strong work ethic. Distribution is a "man's world." So, after 7 years at the company, I made it known that I had my sights on a Regional Operations Manager position. They told me I could possibly be considered for a Regional Customer Service Manager position, which was typically staffed by a woman. After all, they were the same job level and pay grade. And women don't tend to fit in with truck drivers and warehouse people. But I still wanted to be in Operations.

I guess the word got around. After 6 months in my position as Manager of Corporate Operations Auditing, I became the first woman in the company to hold the position of Regional Operations Manager position in the Buena Park, California facility. My hard work and willingness to take lateral positions to expand my knowledge had paid off. But I was even more determined to prove that a woman could effectively work with truck drivers and warehouse people. After all, my mom had worked in a factory for many years, and my dad worked with truck drivers. I felt strongly that my ability to adapt to different situations and people was my best asset.

After a successful eighteen month stint in California (I was awarded the Operations Manager of the Year for Excellence in Inventory Control), I accepted a new position at corporate as the Distribution Liaison in a new marketing group that provided home health care services. This led me into the IT arena while developing a new order entry system for home health patients.

Married to my career....what about my dream?

After nine years, I left to pursue a position at a hospital supply company as an IT Consultant in the Inventory Systems area; it was a new situation and a new challenge. Sound familiar? At the age of 33, I was married to my career and wondering if I would ever fulfill MY DREAM...to have children. Of course, getting married would be a good idea. Little did I know that six weeks after starting the new job, I would meet my husband, Joe. Six months later we were engaged; and eight months later we were married.

Within two years we had our daughter, Liz, who was as precocious as they get. After waiting so long to be a mom, I decided to leave my lucrative full IT position and stay at home. Then one of the managers offered me a position as a contract IT Consultant which would allow me to work part time, 10 hours at home and 10 hours at the office. It was perfect!

Three years later came David, a sensitive young boy with energy beyond compare. At age 3, after three trips to the ER for head injuries and stitches, we had David evaluated for ADHD. Although he was too young to be officially diagnosed, the signs were there. Joe and I started our family so late that we felt totally blessed to have two healthy children, a boy and a girl.

We thought our perfect family was complete. Then three years after David was born, at the age of 43, I was once again blessed with our sweet daughter Michelle. Who knew how much she would shape our lives for many years to come?

She doesn't fit in any box

When Michelle was born I noticed some physical signs that she might have Down syndrome. She wasn't even 5 hours old when the pediatrician walked into my hospital room (and without my husband present), gave me a one minute speech saying that our daughter had Down syndrome, and I shouldn't expect too much from her. She had poor muscle tone, and probably wouldn't walk till she was three or older. Her speech would be delayed, her academic skills would be well behind her peers, and she would probably never be able to take care of herself. At least that is what I remember as he continued talking and I went into a state of numbness. But, before he could run out the door, the phone rang. He reiterated the same monotone, insensitive message to my husband. Okay, so I broke down in tears. While delivering the message to my husband, the pediatrician quickly mentioned something about a possible heart murmur and walked out the door. The entire interaction took less than 10 minutes, yet it turned my life upside down.

I was alone in my hospital room waiting for my husband to find care for our two older children so he could return to the hospital and help me make sense of what had just occurred. I am a very strong person and can handle almost anything thrown at me. When I initially noticed that our daughter had specific physical characteristics that are common with children who have Down syndrome, I knew our lives would change. But, hearing the doctor's matter-of-fact statements made our daughter's future seem hopeless. My husband and I loved her unconditionally and would face the challenges to together.

> "If a child cannot learn in the way we teach...
> We must teach in a way the child can learn."
>
> ~ Ivar Lovaas

Knowledge is power

After lengthy conversations with my husband and countless family and friends, I developed a renewed sense of optimism. During the months that followed I joined a local Down syndrome parent group, joined their Board of Directors, and conducted endless research at the library and on the internet, which, 20 years ago, was in its infancy. I realized something I already knew...our daughter was an individual, NOT Down syndrome. DS was an aspect of who she was, but did not define her entire being.

At a time when most children with DS had to wait to begin Early Intervention until they were 6 months old, I took action and advocated for Michelle to begin at 2 months old. Not only did she crawl at 6 months, she sat at 8 months and walked at 19 months, reaching milestones far ahead of what the doctor had predicted. Why? Because that's what we expected of her. We did not limit her because of some outdated statistics. At 18 months, we left the doctor's practice because they refused to refer us to an ENT to consider ear tubes because of constant congestion. Once the tubes were inserted, Michelle started to walk with assistance and her speech blossomed.

The transformative mom

I continued to work at my "day job" as a contract IT consultant. But it became apparent that I was developing strong advocacy skills during Michelle's preschool years. I continued to educate myself on special education law, attending training programs and supporting other parents with their struggles in the education arena. Not long after Michelle entered an Early Childhood Program at the age of 3, our son David, then 7, was officially diagnosed with ADHD. Reseach into ADHD made me clearly aware that I too may have the condition. A formal evaluation confirmed my suspicions and also helped me understand the many struggles I had since childhood - struggles that also created tremendous challenges for me in college. I wasn't a college dropout. I simply wasn't prepared to handle the demands of college and my life as the "other parent" due to my ADHD. It was a major load off my mind. With maturity I had developed coping skills to deal with my condition. But once diagnosed, I began a medication regime that changed my life forever.

Having two children with disabilities, I was forced to face a battle on two fronts. Once the advocacy skills took hold, it was remarkable to see the transformative effect it had on me as a mother at school meetings and in other areas of my children's lives. Becoming an effective advocate taps into that basic parental instinct to preserve and promote your child's best interest. For this mom, when my children's futures were jeopardized, my basic primal instincts emerged. Mess with me, but don't mess with my kids! Once this transformation occurred, I knew I would never be the same. It unleashed the power of knowing I had a voice, untapped resources available to me, and the ability to make a positive impact on the life of my children. Becoming an effective advocate was a life altering experience for me, my husband and children, and others who have been in contact with me.

Together we can make a difference

It was like someone lit a fire in my belly. The more I learned about my children's educational rights, the more I realized that I could no longer fight this battle in my free time. I made a drastic decision; and with my husband's blessing left my lucrative day job for a year to focus all of my energy on becoming the best advocate I could for my children. When I spoke to other members of my Down syndrome parent group, I continued to hear about the injustices their children were experiencing, and how this negatively impacted the development of their children with DS. I knew we needed to band together in order to make an impact. I partnered with Mary Turon, a DS Board Member, and we intensified our resolve to advocate for other children and support their parents in the process. We attended training programs on reading, math, handwriting, communication methods and special education law and advocacy. On our own we struggled against the system. But, together we made a difference.

> *The thing that makes advocacy such a powerful movement is the inner commitment, the passion of the people for good.*
>
> ~~ *Burton Blatt*

So many gifts still unopened

One year and then two, three, four, but I never went back to that lucrative day job as a contract IT consultant. I continued to volunteer as an advocate for children at school meetings and to give Down Syndrome Disability Awareness presentations to the general education classrooms where my daughter was integrated for Science and

Social Studies. I shared the concept that children with Down syndrome are more like typically developing children than they are different. An amazing transformation occurred in those classrooms. The children to whom I spoke "got it" and shared it with their parents! Soon teachers who had other students with disabilities (Down syndrome, autism) integrated in their classrooms, invited me to talk to their students. I began to realize the broader definition of advocacy. I had been placing my sole energy into each child that I advocated for at their school meetings. Community advocacy allowed me to have a greater impact by changing how people viewed our children with disabilities - not by what they couldn't do, but what they were capable of accomplishing.

> *"All kids are gifted. Some just open their packages earlier than others."*
>
> *-Michael Carr*

Discovering my purpose...not just a dream

Who knew that one short email would change my life forever? A parent from another Down syndrome support group sent me an email asking if I was familiar with the Lake County Center for Independent Living, a non-profit agency that provided services to people with disabilities. 'Of course,' I replied, 'it's about a mile from my house.' It seems they had an open position for a Parent Advocate.

I immediately contacted the Center Director, whom I'd had met previously when our Down syndrome group attended a workshop at the Center. She confirmed that they were accepting applications for a Parent Advocate. She encouraged me to mail a copy of my resume saying he would be in touch. I spent that evening and into the wee hours of the morning revising my once "corporate focused" resume into a document with a focus on advocacy and public service. I hand delivered the cover letter and resume to the Director the following morning. Of course she insisted she would "get back to me" when they had reviewed all of the applications and were ready to schedule interviews.

That was early July, 2003. I stopped by to check in with the Director every week from then until late September when they finally called me for an interview. Then after two grueling interviews I got "the call." The final choice was between me and another candidate. They chose the other candidate because she had more knowledge of special education law. But because they were aware that I had previous experience in financial systems from my corporate days, offered me a position in their financial department. I graciously declined, stating strongly that 'I wanted to be an advocate,' and that I would continue to fulfill that role as a volunteer.

Before I received the email in July I wasn't even aware that someone could actually get paid to be a Parent Advocate. Disappointed, but not beaten, I decided to investigate other opportunities like the position at the Center. By now my husband was urging me to figure out a way to get paid for all the "volunteer" advocacy I was providing. But only a week after I had been told I wasn't chosen for the Parent Advocate position, I received a call from the Director at the Center. She told me that the person who had been selected for the position contacted her the first day she was to report for work to decline the position. Then the Director floored me when she asked, "Are you still interested in the position?" So I held my breath…counted to five…and calmly replied, "Of course I am. Advocacy is my passion!"

I spent the next 5 years at the Center providing educational advocacy to families, teaching students with disabilities employment readiness skills, moderating disability awareness programs in schools all over the Lake County, and promoting community advocacy by working with parents to establish parent groups at their school districts to support and educate families. I also dabbled in "systemic advocacy." This meant trips to the state capital with people with disabilities to speak to lawmakers about supporting legislation that promoted the independence of people with disabilities in their own communities. It was like I discovered a new dimension. With each experience I grew more focused and it became clear that I had found my purpose...not just my dream! But, as time went on, I spent less of my time being a Parent Advocate. My position had grown and the demands of teaching students and organizing activities took its toll on me.

In order to fully support the families on my caseload, I began taking files home to review at night and made calls to parents after hours. The stress became too much. With much I trepidation I approached my husband about the possibility of leaving the Center and opening my own private advocacy practice. This would mean I would be giving up my regular salary (not large by corporate standards, but a salary nonetheless). Without hesitation he supported my new venture responding, "Of course you should do this, it's your passion!"

Three weeks before my fifth anniversary at the Center, I handed in my resignation and never looked back. The next Monday I was "open for business." I sat at the desk in my home office designing forms, researching marketing strategies, and organizing my new business. I decided to call it "From Advocacy to Action," because I felt it communicated the idea of advocating for students by taking the necessary action to improve their educational programming.

But that first morning in my new, very quiet office, I wondered, "Will anyone call?" At 1:00 the phone rang and the person on the other end asked, "Are you a Parent Advocate? If so, I need your help." This was the first sign that I had made the right decision.

For the next six months my practice grew slowly as I received calls from parents I had supported at the Center, and new parents referred by families I supported over the past five plus years. I set a goal of thirty clients the first year. In six months I had sixteen. I was half way to my goal. I conducted Parent workshops on a variety of topics including parents' and students' rights, negotiation, accommodations, etc. and loved every minute. I was unaware that there was a detour in my future, one I could never have predicted.

ad-vo-cate

- *Verb, transitive. To speak, plead or argue in favor of. Synonym is support.*

- *One that argues for a cause; a supporter or defender; an advocate of civil rights.*

- *One that pleads in another's behalf; an intercessor; advocates for children.*

Journey takes a side trip.

Six months after I opened my new practice a neighbor invited me to participate in a small business networking group. One of the members with an Occupational Therapy and Speech/Language practice hosted an Open House and invited the members of the network to attend. Though I was unable to attend the event, shortly after the event, a member contacted me asking whether I knew Charlie Fox, the Special Education Attorney. I knew he was well respected. Apparently his office assistant had attended the event and had a conversation about my role as an advocate. Charlie wanted to meet me for lunch.

First was the lunch; then an invitation to participate in a monthly discussion with other advocates and attorneys, and finally a casual lunch with Charlie to see how I was doing. Charlie offered me a position as an advocate at his law firm. I was flabbergasted! What person in my position would turn down the opportunity to get the experience and exposure that was possible working in a law firm? This was not just any law firm; it is led by someone who is well respected in the special education legal circles.

Though I told Charlie I needed to discuss this opportunity with my husband, I already knew my answer. I couldn't believe this was happening to me! After 11 months in private practice I had exceeded my annual goal by supporting thirty-two clients and was now ready for a new challenge

When life gives you lemons

During my two and a half years at the law office I expanded my advocacy services from two counties to five, and continued presenting workshops to parents. I was exposed to due process cases, had the opportunity to co-present with our associate attorney at a national conference, and took on the role of office coordinator.

I supervised a part time office staff and a part time student who was learning employment skills. Although I had the skill set to handle the duties I had acquired, I realized that I was heading toward the same situation that I experienced at the Center just years before. Because of my additional office duties, I wasn't able to organize and present workshops to families.

I believed it was critical to get the word out to parents who weren't aware of their rights and who hadn't developed the skills to advocate for their children. My role was not only to advocate for children, but also to model those skills so parents could also become effective advocates for their children.

In turn, those same parents would model those advocacy skills for their children so they could become as independent as possible and speak for themselves. Although I was working on many different types of cases directly, and collaborating with the attorneys on so many more, I began to question if I had "sold out" my true passion of being an advocate and nothing else.

In the fall of 2011, the beginning of my third year at the law office, our daughter Michelle became extremely ill, stopped eating and talking and lost a great deal of weight. She was hospitalized for three weeks and was placed on tube feedings. My husband had been laid off from work just days before this started and was spending days at the hospital.

I would come to the hospital after work and spend the night. In the morning my husband would show up with my clean clothes and we would start all over again. It was an extremely stressful time for our family. My daughter came home from the hospital and attended school half days. My husband started a new job, so we needed to find caregivers to feed and care for Michelle in the afternoon till we arrived home from work.

In the midst of this, Charlie decided to move our office to a building a few suburbs away. Coordinating the move in the midst of my daughter's illness was almost my undoing. Michelle had developed extreme anxiety regarding the passing periods at school. It was difficult to handle too many people and too much noise, plus a fear that someone would "bump into her tube. So, we made the decision to replace the larger tube with one that was smaller and less obtrusive. Little did we know that this "simple" outpatient procedure would create such havoc and almost end our daughter's life!

In late January Michelle had an outpatient procedure to replace her tube. Everything went without a hitch. Or so we thought. Upon returning home Michelle refused to allow us to feed her using her new tube. The doctor suggested an over the counter pain reliever and fever reducer. By that evening Michelle had a fever of 102°. The second day she was still not eating. On the third day we took Michelle to the Down Syndrome Clinic.

After a brief exam the nurse sent us immediately to the emergency room at the hospital. Michelle's heart rate was extremely high from sepsis, a serious life threatening infection caused by the tube being placed in the peritoneum cavity instead of the stomach. Two days later, after an unsuccessful attempt to clear the infection, Michelle was taken into emergency surgery. She spent two days in ICU and an additional two and half weeks in the hospital.

From the time Michelle was admitted to the hospital until she was released to come home, I only left her side twice, and then my husband was by her side. I did what I could to support the families for whom I advocated. They were all very understanding and rescheduled meetings or had me participate by phone when it was possible. They understood my priority was my daughter's health. I continued to support the office staff in every way possible.

My second year at the law office Charlie gave me a birthday gift which was a 70's vintage type of clock. It had the outline of a person floating in the air holding ribbons with wings at the ends. The inscription on the clock read, "Sometimes you must jump off the cliff and build your wings on the way down". That is exactly what I had done when I left the Center to pursue my private practice of advocacy. I placed the clock on the wall in my kitchen next to the sink as a daily reminder.

During those many hours in that hospital room I thought about the five months since my daughter became ill. I realized how challenging it was try and focus on her and work at the law office. By the time my daughter finally was able to return home I knew what I had to do.

Spirit renewed

The week Michelle returned home I contacted Charlie at the law office. Charlie needed to be able to rely on someone to be in the office and to coordinate the office activities. And I needed to be available to support my daughter as she returned home and to her school activities. My daughter was my first priority. Beyond that, all I wanted was my clients and to be an advocate. I did not want to coordinate the office activities. We agreed to send out a letter to all of my clients asking them to choose between coming with me and remaining as a client of the law office. Of the forty plus clients I was supporting, all but a few chose to leave the practice and join me in my private practice. Within two months my clients had signed releases for their records, and I was attending school meetings that had been scheduled and rescheduled due to my daughter's hospital stay. From Advocacy to Action was back in business.

Over the next several months my daughter continued to be my main priority. I was home when she left for school and home when she returned in the afternoon. If a meeting went late, my son would be home to greet her. I finally had control of my schedule and my time so I could be there when she needed me.

I would never want to have my daughter go through that experience again. She almost lost her life. I am simply grateful that I was able to see clearly, knowing that her health and her life were a priority. And in the end I was available to advocate for her medical needs as well. This experience tested our family, but also brought us closer together.

Life's passion

It has been over 2 ½ years since I left the law office. I have never looked back on my decision. Charlie and I maintain a professional relationship. I continue to refer clients to his office and remain involved in the advocate/attorney monthly group where he is a member. After not eating or talking for 8 months, our daughter started to eat solids and her speech returned. She attended her high school graduation and started to attend a Transition program in the fall of 2012.

Meanwhile my practice has continued to grow and flourish, allowing me the opportunity to take on a limited number of Pro Bono cases. I have time to return to presenting workshops to parents. In 2013 I was enrolled in a yearlong special education advocate certification program with forty-four other participants, which included a practicum under the supervision of a special education attorney. It was a mind blowing experience I will never forget. Since I didn't have a college degree, this certification, along with fourteen years of experience, finally legitimized me as an advocate.

Throughout the process I have networked with interesting and talented people who have created new professional connections for me. Artist Jeane Heckert developed a logo for my practice and then designed a website that truly captured my life's passion to advocate for others and teach them to do the same.

Our daughter became ill again in the fall of 2013 and was hospitalized in December. She continues to struggle with the same issues that caused her problems in 2011-12; and we are doing everything we can to encourage her eating solids and talking again.

In early September, 2013 our son, only 22 at the time, was diagnosed with testicular cancer. He had successful surgery and is doing well. He was married on September 14, 2014 just a year after his diagnosis.

When my children became ill there was no question about my priorities. But I do know that being in private practice gave me the freedom to be there for them. It allows me to continue to pursue my life's passion, to advocate for children with disabilities and their families. My life is truly blessed!

Hundred Years

A hundred years from now
it will not matter
what my bank account was,
the sort of house I lived in,
or the kind of car I drove
but the world
may be different
because I was important
in the life of a child.

~ Forest Witcraft

There is still more work to be done. I have renewed energy to continue my efforts to support and educate families. The thought of retirement is not even in view. I have been seeking out others who have the same philosophy and passion that I possess for the work I've been blessed to do. Until then I will continue my work as a Special Education Advocate.

A special thank you

I want to thank my husband Joe for his continued encouragement to pursue my passion. I also want to thank my daughter Liz and my son David who believed in me and my ability to provide families with the guidance and support they needed to advocate for their children with special needs. Most of all I want to thank my daughter Michelle whose courage and determination continue to amaze me every day as she deals with the challenges of her developmental disability. She is my hero and gives me purpose for the work I am blessed to do.

About Pam

Pam Labellarte has been married to her husband Joe for 30 years. She has three children, Liz 28, Dave, 24 and Michelle, 21. Pam has been providing Special Education Advocacy services in Northern Illinois and Southern Wisconsin for 15 years, and since 2009 through her private practice, From Advocacy to Action. Pam can be reached at plabellarte@gmail.com
847-401-5053
www.fromadvocacy2action.com

And Sew it Went

By Linda Polhemus, Custom Window Treatment Designer

Looking back, it is much easier to see why you end up doing what you do in life. I never would have made my current career a goal, or guessed how I would get here!

First love — could it be fabric?

My love affair with fabric and creating things with it began early. Making clothes for my Barbie and Troll dolls was the beginning. Then in Junior High a whole new world opened up in Home Ec. Class with Mrs. McMichaels. She was a Southern lady with a knockout figure (not what you'd think of when you thought of a Home Ec. teacher). When I realized I could expand my wardrobe by making my own clothes, I was in heaven! The fact that my mother willingly purchased fabric for my productive hobby was also a plus!

Another inspiration was my High School Home Ec. Teacher, Mrs. Hornberger. I wanted to be her! As a senior she taught flat patterning and advanced tailoring where we made 100% wool coats and learned the intricacies of interlining, padding and bound buttonholes, for starters. Those who were interested could enter the local competition. So I did and won! Then I went on to be victorious at the county competition too.

My first mentor

Also at the competition was my Mother. No story about me would be complete without acknowledging her love and support throughout my life. My Mom, Ruth, was the first woman to attend college in her family: and it was on a scholarship to Temple University, no less. My parents divorced when I was 5. So as a single mom she moved us in with my Grandmother. Since we shared a bedroom, my Grandmother made the back porch her bedroom.

My Mom borrowed money from her Uncle for a car and clothes, got a teaching job in the Philadelphia school system, and took care of us. When I was 9 she married a wonderful man that we lost just 5 years later at 38 to cancer. We were on our own again. Ruth was then married to Bob for 33 years. Even during the tough times she saved the $70/ month support from my father; so when I graduated from high school, she could pay for my four years at a private college. Actually she said, "You can get a job, or you can go to college." What a choice!

She has always been hardworking and determined, and passed on her love of learning and all things interesting to me! She taught me that no matter what life tosses your way, you pick yourself up and make a life! I know that watching her dedication to her students, her passion for learning, her zest for life, and her love for our family helped shape the person I am today.

Lessons for life from college

It seemed an easy decision to go to Valparaiso University and earn a BS in Home Economics Education. I loved the diverse subjects that were part of my program, and did well. Student teaching was daunting and exhausting. Having only cooking classes to teach was a little disappointing too made all the more challenging because the senior girls and boys in this small Indiana town questioned my authority.

Since I was only a few years their senior (so they said), and a couple of them were soon going to be parents, they felt they knew better than me about what they'd be putting on their tables. Beer bottle caps would periodically fly onto my desk...an eye opening preview of the kinds of kids I would be teaching.

Sorry, no teachers needed

With college over way too soon, it was back to Pennsylvania where I began searching for a Home Ec teaching job in the PA/NJ area. I quickly realized that in Jr. or Sr. High Schools there were several math science and English teachers, but only one, maybe two, Home Ec teachers. (Why were we not told this?) On top of that, add the glut of teacher graduates in the late 70s.

Fortunately, I did a very smart thing in high school. I learned to type. During college I had great summer temp jobs in various offices. I spent two summers at a large pharmaceutical company where it was a privilege to have a 9-5 full time job.

After college, I worked at a computer maintenance company in King of Prussia, PA while looking for a teaching position. When my job search failed to land a teaching position, the company hired me as a full-time secretary in the Marketing Department. After being shuffled around several times, I was put at a desk and told to 'look busy.' I don't do this well; I need to be doing something meaningful.

At age 23 I was looking for another job when I answered an ad for a Regional Administrator position with a reprographics (copier) company. No one was more surprised than I when I got the job. I worked for the Regional Sales manager and traveled the eastern part of the country hiring and training field office secretaries. I also traveled to the Chicago headquarters to meet with other RA's and write procedures for the company offices. Here I was using my teaching and organizational abilities! It was a great job. But the biggest benefit was meeting my husband, Barry, who also worked in the Regional office.

Let's move to Chicago!

When we got married in October we knew that Barry had a new job in Chicago starting in December of 1983. It was a great career move for Barry, but not for me. My job was not transferable. So when we got to Chicago I began life as a leasing coordinator, which was not-my-favorite-job. (Please read between the lines). Then something even more life changing happened. We found out we were going to have our first child.

Moving to Chicago was an adventure. I had some friends in the area from college that I'd see from time to time. But we had to make a new life, away from all family. We joined a wonderful church, made friends and found our place in the Midwest!

Later, when I realized we would have TWO children in the space of 15 months, I changed my job description to Full-Time Mom.

Linda's Custom Sewing is born

Life with toddlers was busy, but I felt the need to contribute to the family budget, and missed the challenges of having a job. So I did office work on the side for a CPA, did some child care for other moms, and kept sewing. At this point sewing was still my private passion. I was used to making a lot of my own clothes, and I then began to make clothes for my boys. I also made curtains and bedding for their nurseries.

A move to a new home inspired me to get serious about decorating my windows. I had done a few things in our first home. The gradual transition from making mainly clothing to making some window treatments had me learning again. People noticed what I was doing, and asked if I sewed for others.

During this time, we added Amy to our family. Now we had 3 children. It was wonderful to have a little one again, and to be working and doing something I loved.

Soon I was sewing for friends and people they referred to me but without a clue about what to charge. So I charged by the hour. This is when the light bulb went on in my head, or as my business coach now calls it, "a blinding flash of the obvious." I could make money doing what I loved! The skill that I had was marketable. Barry made an upstairs bedroom into my sewing room, and then when our boys wanted their own rooms, he moved it to the biggest room and I shared it with my son. I passed out flyers in mailboxes during this time, and actually got a couple of clients.

One notable job started out as a drapery project for a couple of opera singers, but grew to include alterations on the wife's gowns. I was asked to make a black lace top with a purple underlay for an existing gown; and I had to do it while she was away. My stomach turned over the day I bought the $100/yard lace to start the project. But what a thrill it was working on her gowns. My most famous piece was actually worn on stage at the New York Metropolitan Opera.

They say timing is everything. Talk about being in the right place at the right time. I was using a sewing machine repair shop in Lake Zurich, when the owner learned that I had a small sewing business going. He was thrilled to find me. Apparently, the phone book had made a mistake in his listing saying he did alterations, which he certainly did not.

He immediately began funneling all such calls to me, and suddenly I was busy with alterations and other sewing projects for people.

I continued to enjoy the drapery projects more than the clothing. Believe me, doing alterations can kill you, especially where brides, wedding parties and mothers are concerned. There was one woman that had lost about 50 pounds, and had me take in every piece of clothing she owned. Despite working with her nicotine infused garments, it was wonderful getting a paycheck.

But I enjoyed the fresh new fabrics the most! When people brought me beautiful prints to make pillows or valances, I was in heaven! A mix of projects kept me increasingly busier, so I called myself "Linda's Custom Sewing" for the next 11 years. The growth in my business necessitated a move into the basement, where there was more room for my "hobby turned business venture."

Designing women

Along the way, I was meeting people all the time. (I now realize this was networking.) My realtor introduced me to a designer, and I began fabricating her window treatments. She took me to the Merchandise Mart where I discovered the beautiful fabric showrooms. She suggested that I sign up with a fabric company and get some of their basic sample fabric books so I would have a selection of fabrics to show our clients and my customers. I quickly learned that I could make money from offering fabric to clients, instead of them buying the supplies and bringing them to me. That's also when I realized that I needed to have a "real business" to have accounts with vendors.

So we started this process, and I began acquiring suppliers. Beautiful fabric books arrived on my doorstep books I could keep and look at and share! I was in heaven! Now I needed more storage. Barry brought in book cases and put a computer under the stairs for me.

I was in the routine of being Mom in the morning, working during school hours, and then back to carpool and school activities. Then at night I would retreat into the basement and work. I knew this was the only space that would work for me and the business, but it was not ideal. I froze in the summer when the AC was on, and also in the winter, when I used a space heater. I really had no thoughts about alternative work space, because there was none. I had to put the cutting surface on the pool table to work, and then remove it when the kids wanted to play pool.

About this time, I found out about the Window Fashions Certification Program. I began taking classes at the seminars offered once a year when they came to Chicago. I studied and took the tests, and met a lot of people who had businesses like mine. I learned that making draperies is only part of the window covering process, and that I was leaving money on the table. If I could offer hard window treatments to my clients (blinds and shades), I could make them very happy AND increase my profit as well. I began selling shades and learning all about "inside mount" vs. "outside mount," energy efficiency, and what kinds of shades work in what applications.

A new name, a new direction

I began to think that I needed a different name for my business, because I was now ready to advertise! I was still doing some clothing, but increasingly more home decorating. So in 2000, the name "Custom Sewing Innovations" seemed appropriate. I hired one of my clients to design a logo, and got business cards and letterhead. Advertising in the local women's club newsletter brought me more clients to add to my neighbors and their friends.

In 2004, I became a member of the Window Coverings Association of America. By attending their monthly meetings I was learning more about the industry all the time. I became a dealer for Hunter Douglas, and also began carrying more fabric lines and drapery hardware. I worked during the day, scheduled appointments around my children's activities, and went out at night to see clients when my husband was home.

I must give credit to my husband for being the best guy in the world. Through the years, he always supported my efforts. He was there to build me a sewing center in a bedroom, and then suggest my move to the basement when I needed more room. (I actually hated that idea, because I felt I was going "underground," which I was). But he made it as nice as he could for me, finishing the basement and building yet another sewing center. When I brought home more samples, he'd build another rack, and we'd figure out which part of the house I could take over next.

Barry was also my installer for most of my career. He would work all week, then go installing with me in the evenings and on weekends. He built cornice boxes, cut boards, hung blinds, drilled holes, and made my creations look beautiful! I am certain that because of the way he anchored my treatments to the walls, houses would fall down long before my drapes would. I am forever indebted to him for his support, hard work and determination to give me what I needed to enable me to turn my passion into a business that I love!

Movin' on up

Eventually the day came when we reached our breaking point. Custom Sewing Innovations was outgrowing the limits of our home, and I was losing my mind spending so much of my life "underground." Carrying samples up stairs and into the car and then back down again was difficult; and there was nowhere else to go with the samples!

In 2006, after weighing the possibilities of renting a retail space vs. building onto our home, we decided to build the addition. It would allow me to do my business and still be there for our children every day, which was a priority for us. We turned our 3 car garage into my work room and showroom, and added a 3 car garage to our home for the vehicles. After a six month renovation, I can still remember the first day the builders brought my sewing machines upstairs. I demanded the move. It was taking so long!

"Get me up there; I am for sure going to lose my mind if I am in this basement for one more day!" I said. It was my birthday, it was raining, and it was wonderful! My cutting table was on sawhorses for a while longer, but I was "in the light!"

A funny thing happened with the move. I looked more professional and felt more professional. It gave my business a whole new legitimacy. When clients came, they no longer had to go down into my basement. I had a dedicated space.

I started getting more business, and soon needed help. My friend Kellie was my first helper. She was fantastic and had a similar Home Ec background; but between full-time jobs, she could not stay on part time. We worked well together. It was a nice way to become used to sharing my space and having help. When Kellie left, I continued to need more help. Not long after that, Donna, a fellow church member, came to work for me.

Plugging into the network

Then I discovered networking. Of all places, I was at church with my blind samples, intending to help solve the light control issues in our new sanctuary with screen roller shades. Frank, a fellow parishioner there, asked what I was doing, so I explained my business. He invited me to a networking meeting. I was pretty scared, but went; and then I went back again. Next thing I knew, I had joined!

Networking meetings helped me to grow. I learned to stand up in front of people every week and tell them what I did. I learned that if I educated my networking "sales team," they could tell other people what I do, and recommend my services to them, just as I was learning to do the same thing for them. It worked! Plus, I met friends that had businesses that would help my business grow! Christa helped me design a new brochure and web site; Kathy helped me write the copy and found me a photographer to take beautiful pictures of my work to use; and Gerry (CPA) helped me redefine my business. I met people I could trust and refer to my clients. So I became a valuable contact, AND we all had fun! I also joined the local Chamber of Commerce.

Over the last few years, I accepted several networking leadership roles, and also served as VP of the Chicago Chapter of the WCAA. All of these opportunities have added to my knowledge and confidence along the way. I've learned the value of associations and networking, and appreciate the relationships I have with so many wonderful people. I am challenged every day with aspects of my business. And it is still growing! In fact, I've started business coaching with the idea that I can make it even better.

We have recently changed our DBA to WINDOW TREATMENTS BY DESIGN, which better represents our place in the industry and the services we offer to our clients. I have hired an administrator to take me away from the bills and paperwork, and have initiated marketing programs and more aggressive social media activity. I am taking the time to define and refine the operation, so when I'm ready I'll have a valuable business I can sell.

When asked what I would have done differently, it's hard to say. Maybe I would have gone the route of interior designer instead of getting a BS in Home Ec Education. But back then I couldn't have known I'd be where I am today. My business has evolved with me. Where would I be now? Who knows? I feel blessed that I could have it all - a great husband, three wonderful children, and a profession that is my passion! I know I've been on the path I was meant to travel, and am grateful for it and for everyone that helped and inspired me along the way.

More about Linda

Linda is the owner of Window Treatments by Design based in the northwest suburbs of Chicago. She and husband Barry are the parents of three grown children who were raised amid bolts of fabrics, several cats and a beloved dog named Snickers.

Website: www.windowtreatmentsbydesign.com
Email: lindapsewitwent@gmail.com
Facebook: Window Treatments by Design

Lunges of Faith

By Bonnie Richtman, Business/Cognitive Skills Coach

I

I am a "Corporate America Child." What does that mean? It means that I worked in a large corporation. That's pretty much where I received most of my training in the business world.

Who am I? My name is Bonnie Richtman. I am one of three children--the Middle Child: supposedly, the most well-adjusted since I had to get along with both a big brother *and* a little sister. Constantly adjusting to the changes from the role of eldest daughter to little sister was interesting training, I should say, and somehow very relevant at that.

I grew up in a household where money was scarce. Oh, we had everything we needed and I didn't really feel the lack of funds. However, I knew my mother was on a pretty tight budget which was reinforced regularly with, "we can't afford that" when we requested the typical new and mostly unnecessary baubles that most children of my era pleaded for.

My generation was really one of the first in which girls really had an open door to attend college. Most of our mothers had never attended, and certainly few grandmothers had. I still lived in an environment where education for the girl was considered a luxury and not a necessity—at least that's the way it was in my immediate environment.

My mother and father, having limited resources, made it quite clear that if they were to manage college for any of their three children, it would be their son; because, they reasoned, he would have to one day support a family. The girls, they figured, would most likely become wives and mothers and have husbands to support them. So educating them was lower on their priority list.

As a result, I didn't think college for me was important. Although I liked school and did well, I just assumed that I wouldn't go on to a secondary education. Truthfully, I loved the social aspect of school more than I did the academics anyway.

Now, keep in mind that this is my own perception. My younger sister would beg to differ. She did attend college and would not settle for anything less than the education she felt she was entitled to. Somehow I missed that memo. I did not feel entitled. I did not feel entitled at all. Truth be told, and this is hard for me to admit out loud, but…here goes: at my deepest core I did not believe that I was college material. I feared that I would fail, that I was not smart enough, that I was not good enough. If I tried college and failed, then everyone would know. Everyone would know… Nope, better to get married and have children. After all, isn't that what was expected of me anyway?

So, I married young. In the end that proved to be a disaster. It took me 34 years and hours of therapy to realize it, but that's a whole other story.

II

Before I lead you to think my LIFE was a disaster, let me assure you that it wasn't. That union produced five beautiful, wonderful human beings. I consider it one my greatest fortunes and my greatest honor to be called "Mother" by each one of them. And I learned a great deal along the way. So you see my life was not a disaster. My marriage was, as it turned out, but certainly not my life.

Let's see, where to start with this piece of my story? Hmmm, let's begin in 2004.

I met her at the bus stop. Rhonda was nervously standing there, fussing over her first born daughter who was about to hop on the big yellow school bus and head to her first day of a brand new school after moving into a brand new neighborhood. Rhonda's second daughter, a little one, was all snuggled up and cozy in a stroller. Rhonda's eldest was the same age as my youngest.

My kids and I and the newcomers exchanged perfunctory "hellos," and received nods and smiles in return. The girls, excited about their first day of school, hit it off immediately. Of course that formed a bond between us moms. After a few weeks of bus-stop chatting, Rhonda and I became fast friends.

Rhonda was a Physical Therapist by trade. She was an educated woman who knew her craft and, quite honestly, had an incredible gift for diagnostics in the Physical Therapy realm. Rhonda was living her calling.

After getting to know one another we discovered, among other things, that we were both concerned about health in general, which included the same thoughts about the importance of exercise. The next logical step unfolded and we started to take long walks together in the mornings after the school bus collected our children. It was on these walks that we shared our life's hopes and dreams.

I learned that Rhonda's dream was to open her own Physical Therapy Clinic, and Rhonda learned that I had always dreamed of owning my own business.

After 10 years in Corporate America, I became more and more frustrated that I could not invest in my office and my employees the way I wanted to. There was always some person several states away that had the authority to make or break my plans. Corporate decisions were based on the company as a whole, as it should be. However, I did not like being accountable for other branches of our firm where I had no influence on how they were running and managing their resources.

As other parts of the company experienced losses, my office was experiencing gains. To keep the company as a whole solvent, Corporate directed all offices across the board to cut expenses. That meant jobs, salaries, support, equipment, education etc. would be impacted. Though I understood the effort was to help offset our counterparts that were not producing, frankly, I didn't much like it.

It seemed no matter how hard I worked, I could not reward my employees for a job well done when tied to a budget that was predicated on things over which I had no control. There was no budget for education, bonuses, job promotions, vacations, celebrations, benefits and the like. No money for innovation. No money for upgrading equipment, products or services. No money for anything that was unique to my market or my market niche.

Everything was uniform regardless of the miles separating our unique situations. If a branch half-way across the nation wasn't doing well, I felt completely tied because my office had to help make up their deficit. I understood why Corporate made its decisions. I just didn't like being excluded from decision processes that had profound effects on my branch.

I wanted to open my own business for many reasons, one of which was autonomy so I could take care of my employees the way I envisioned it. I wanted to make my office a great place to work, where everyone enjoyed their job and found it satisfying to be there. I wanted to be able to embrace the community by offering support in philanthropic venues that support my values. I feel very strongly that it is imperative we support our communities and local businesses.

As a result, my money is infused into local companies every chance I get---even if it costs me a little more out of pocket to do so. I am a firm believer in investing both time and money in one's community. How wonderful it would be to be in a position to not only follow that line of thought myself but to be able to offer that freedom to my employees as well.

I just couldn't hold true and follow through with these ideals in a corporate setting.

III

So, after many conversations, some brain storming sessions, a few glasses of wine, some laughs, some worry, some blockades, some tears, some more glasses of wine and some very late nights, the concept of Rhonda's and my business was born.

We would be the "go to" clinic in town. We would dedicate ourselves to the promise that our patients are the number one priority in all aspects of their care. We would be family friendly; children of patients would not only be welcomed, they would have a nice place to play so we could keep a watchful eye on them while their parents were undergoing treatment.

Rhonda and I would go the extra mile for each patient regardless of the time or the cost involved. Sometimes that meant driving a patient home after an appointment if a ride was needed. Sometimes it meant detecting what could be a subtle problem with a patient and acting on intuition. Sometimes it meant rushing a patient directly to the hospital, or coordinating appropriate care with a patient's family or caretaker. Sometimes it meant delivering cars directly to driveways so a discharged hospitalized patient would return home and find their car ready and waiting for normal life to resume. Sometimes it meant visiting someone in the hospital. Or sometimes it simply meant meeting a lonely patient for coffee. We considered our patients "family" and we were dedicated to treating them as such.

Our reception/front office staff were trained and encouraged to visit with patients if the patients were in a chatty mood as they awaited their appointments. We realized that some of our patients, particularly some of our seniors, rarely have social time. Our philosophy was that the work will get done if we all pitch in and help when and where we can. Our office mission, vision, and values embraced teamwork and team spirit. We were a team and we worked as a team. At least that was the goal; and we met that goal most of the time.

We made Physical Therapy easily accessible to everyone by checking insurance coverage and laying out custom budgets that were affordable for each individual patient. We made sure that if someone who was experiencing pain called us, we would evaluate and treat them as soon as humanly possible but absolutely within 24 hours of the phone call. We provided state-of-the-art "Family Friendly" service to each and every visitor, and made every person who entered our doors feel welcomed and cared for.

Later, with the help of our Business Coach, I learned that these beliefs formed our USP (Unique Selling Proposition). Conforming to these values and delivering this to our patients on a consistent basis is what made our clinic stand out.

Our patients felt valued, cared for, and realized improvements with their pain and range of motion. So although there were things we needed to implement too improve our business, there were some things that we were doing very right indeed.

IV

One of the most important things I learned as a Business Owner was that having an unbiased, experienced set of eyes and ears on the outside looking in is a huge advantage. Those of us in the thick of things miss clarity as the day to day issues fog up the scene. When that fog clears away and issues come into focus...well, great things begin to happen and work becomes fun again! The feelings of hope and optimism rush back. Those feelings of that first exhilaration is just as strong or stronger than when we proudly opened the doors to our business that very first time!

Our mission, vision, values and USP were very good and well planned; and providing the very best care for people while genuinely striving to make a positive difference in their lives is a wonderful premise. BUT, (yes, there are always two sides of every story), the other side to that coin is very real—it's called profit. Without profits and revenue you *have* no business – it's that simple. How do you make both sides of that coin shiny? Ahhh, now there's the rub... (No pun intended).

You polish both consistently with vigor. THAT, my friends, is the key to making your business successful. Is it simple? No. Is it easy? No. Is it do-able? Yes! Is it fun? Absolutely!

Especially when you have a cause that tugs at your heartstrings, but the solution is blocked by a big, ugly obstacle. There is no feeling greater than first time you realize that you, you yourself, have the wherewithal to help—the privilege of being able to pull out your checkbook and melt that obstacle into a nothing, my friends. New cars and vacations are nice. But feeding a starving child, providing

Christmas Cheer when it is most needed, funding medical care, educating our children both locally and on a global basis, cleaning up the environment or water supply, or watching the sorrow melt from a mother's eyes as she sees a solution to her child's pain—there are no words. It humbles you and makes you very thankful that you have been blessed so abundantly.

We call that "legacy." It is beautiful. The business has now become a platform.

Amazing things happen as we grow. The world we used to view was 2-Dimensional. When the 3rd dimension is revealed it is mind blowing. I can't wait for the 4th if, indeed, it exists. I had a mentor who used to tell me, "there are bigger things than you or I at work." I listened but I didn't understand what she was saying until years later. Perhaps, as yet, I have only glimpsed a small part of it.

V

I have already mentioned some of the reasons that I wanted to own a business. There are more. I wanted a little freedom and independence in my personal life, both financially and time-wise.

But a tight budget left little opportunity for choice. I envied my friends who had choice. It always seemed that I did what was needed to be done—choice, even with the little things, was non-existent for me. On especially busy nights, did I want to order take-out for dinner to feed my family of 7 instead of further complicating a very full day of activities with cooking? Yes! But that was a choice that I couldn't really make given our financials. With credit card debt and a list of bills that ate up pretty much all of our income, it was hard to justify spending those extra dollars for pre-prepared food.

So, I made it work. As I watched neighbors walk uptown with their families to enjoy a relaxing meal in a restaurant, I envied them. I knew that in addition to all the work and activities that I had with my five children, I would be cooking and cleaning up the kitchen and dining room, and most likely, some floors before the bedtime routine rolled around.

The bedtime routine was not a light endeavor. It meant bathing the children, reading them their bedtime stories, preparing for the early morning school routine, perhaps packing some lunches, tossing a few things in the washing machine etc. before collapsing into bed that night, exhausted, only to repeat that dance again the next day and the next and the next.

A nice, little break from the everyday work, where I could relax and enjoy mealtime and conversation with my family without the impending dirty dishes would have been so nice. All I really wanted was a little help. I put all my hopes in the dream that this business would provide the income I needed so I could make some nice changes in my life: help with the cleaning, some quiet time to read, maybe carve out a little time to exercise. How about a vacation in the sun?

I simply could not relax. All I could see were all the things that needed tending to. There was laundry or cleaning or mending or dishes or dusting or something somewhere that needed attention. Turn a blind eye to it? Out of sight, out of mind? Didn't work for me.

I like beauty. Harmony. If something is out of place I feel it needs to be put in its proper place. That might be a carry-over from mornings frantically searching for shoes. With five little pairs of feet, not being able to quickly locate a shoe meant missing the bus in the morning, or a glove, or a coat, or a lunch box, or homework, or a school book, or a myriad of other things. I think the most common request I heard back in those past days was, "Mom, where is my (you fill in the blank)" and most times I knew the answer. Again, I digress…Now, where was I? Ah, yes.

Many women who aspire to own their own businesses deal with roadblocks that male counterparts don't necessarily experience. I recognize it and understand it because I lived it; and I see other women struggle with those same issues. It can be very difficult in our society to overcome existing stereotypes.

In some cases successful women, or those who dream of being wildly successful, can overwhelm a spouse. I can't fully explain the dynamics because, personally, the concept of holding somebody back is foreign to me. It can be those subtleties that derail to the biggest extent. The big things you can see. They are tangible. You can wrap your arms around them. Those subtleties are hard to grasp. They are like wisps of mist ever changing and shifting with the air currents.

I have felt, and have been told by other Female Business Owners, that these obstacles feel more like imagination than reality. I have been in the coaching room as these women ask the same questions that I asked myself in those wee hours of those long and sleepless nights: "Did that really happen or am I imagining that? Am I nuts? Do I really expect too much? Am I really unreasonable to expect to have a family AND a successful business? It is so crazy to work toward organizing the chaos of a houseful of children AND organizing the chaos of my office?"

Life can be extremely complicated. Don't let someone else derail you. It is truly a birth right to be allowed to strive to become the best that you can be. No one should be able to take that away from you. Isn't that what we fight for here in the United States of America – freedom; freedom to dream; freedom to work hard; freedom to attain what you want if you are willing to pay the price; freedom, no matter what your station in life; freedom to break the chains and break free? Yep, I certainly think so.

VI

The next big hurdle for Rhonda and I was to convince our husbands that we were serious about this business venture. Mine, I believe, thought it was kind of cute, so he would humor me and allow me to pursue this little venture. I don't think my situation is unique. When it comes to actually outlaying a lot of money, it can be a hard sell.

Anyway, I felt that it was finally my turn to do something for myself. I wanted to finish college, but I just didn't have the time to invest in an education for myself. My children were quickly approaching college age and the luxury of time just wasn't there. So my best bet, I believed, was to open this business and, hopefully, earn enough to supplement our income until our finances could improve. This extra income could pay for the kids' upcoming college costs, and give us a little breathing room. I really hoped to earn enough money so I could hire some household help.

I don't remember how we agreed, if we agreed, or if my husband just gave in. Anyway, I got the $12,500 cash which was my half of the $25,000 start-up capital we needed to make our venture a "go."

All the steps we took to open our clinic are the typical steps any start-up would take.

I know it is a little out of order here, but I will tell you, in Year 5 I hired a Business Coach. It changed my life—nearly doubled our clinic's gross revenues in a little less than two years. I wish I would have known to hire a Coach from the get-go. It would have saved us a lot of unnecessary and costly mistakes. The investment in a Coach was well worth every penny as I saw the rate of return on the investment grow! But, this is a little ahead of the story. Stay tuned…

In early 2004, when Rhonda and I were seriously talking about starting our own Physical Therapy Clinic, I heard that the W.E.D.O. (Women's

Economic Development Organization) of our County was hosting a seminar at the Local Junior College. There are some great resources available at no cost designed to help aspiring Business Owners, so do take advantage of them! There were four of us in our little group who attended that seminar. Of the four, only I forged ahead and started a business.

VII

We all know that a large number of business fail every year. Government statistics show that just under 20% of the businesses that start this year will survive to see their 5th year. Only 20% of those will see their 10th anniversary. This means that a whopping 95%-96% of any new business won't make it to their 10 year mark. That's pretty sobering.

At the W.E.D.O. Conference, I met a gentleman from the SBA and learned that I was a Minority Owned Business because ours was a woman owned business. As such, there were programs out there designed to help women like us obtain funding for new business ventures. Too cool! After attending that seminar and taking copious amounts of notes, I met with that gentleman. He gave me some great insights as to what I really had to do and the necessary steps to take to get the necessary funding I would need to make my dream a reality.

I found out that the prerequisite for borrowing money was much more than an idea. Even if that idea was brilliant and extremely well thought out, it was still not enough. You need collateral. Collateral? You basically bet your success on whatever you establish as your collateral. In many cases including mine, people use the equity in their homes. IF your venture does not pan out, and you can't pay your loan back, you could lose your house or whatever you put up for collateral. It is a big risk. Many people are not cut out for this level of risk.

I remember thinking that only people WITH money get the privilege of opening a business. You can't MAKE money unless you HAVE money! How unfair and backward that seemed to me. How do people like me even get started? Are we doomed before we even begin? Where can I get that kind of money since I don't have any assets worth anything? The most valuable things in my life are my children. I can't indenture a child can I? Just kidding…

If I was serious about this, the most logical place to start to get this ball rolling would require the development of a Business Plan. Okay. This takes a dream from thought and concept and lofty ideas to the concrete. Words and numbers on a piece of paper make it real, tangible. Yikes! Where to start?

I did some research and learned that a Business Plan is more involved and intricate than just plugging in some numbers. A good plan should encompass the business as a whole with all its unique facets. Including marketing, market share, competition, cost of production, staffing, contracts, incorporating, the list goes on… complicated, indeed. Like I said, owning a business is not for the fainthearted. But I felt it would be very rewarding.

Okay, a Business Plan. I understand now why this is the first thing you need when planning to open a business. You use it to talk to a bank lender about funding, lines of credit, loans, etc. How can you move forward if you don't have a plan? A plan is a roadmap. You have to know where you want to go before you can even begin the first step on your trip. If you just open your doors without a well thought out plan you are just in chaos; and flying by the seat of your pants just doesn't work. Even with plenty of money coming in the doors, if you don't have a plan, eventually your "house" will fall. And that fall will be great.

My first job was to visit the local library to do some research. I know what you're thinking. Why didn't I just go online? Did I need to go to the Library to borrow a computer to go on line? Nope. In yesteryear… hard to admit…actually kind of embarrassing…no actually very embarrassing I didn't know how to use a computer at that time.

I sat down, once, in front of our home computer, waved my hands around, poked my index finger a little here and there, slapped the keyboard, and cursed at it once or twice, all to no avail. I could not even figure how to turn the darn thing on. I sighed my typical, "I am not technical in any way" sigh, and disgustedly flounced away from that silent, mocking, beast feeling nothing but intense hatred that the world was moving on without me. *What is wrong with paper and pencil anyway?!*

Once I got over that, I went to the card catalogue at my trusty local library and looked up books on starting your own business and creating a business plan. Thankfully the Library has a help desk. The lady was very helpful, understanding and wished me luck. Too cool!

After reading those books, I felt armed to take the next step which included asking other Business Owners for their advice. For the most part they were very willing to share their experiences and ideas which was a real confidence booster!

I was now ready to visit my banker. As he spoke about Margins, Cost of Sales, Fixed Costs, Depreciation, Revenue Cycles, Market Analysis, P&Ls , Balance Statements, tax implications and KPI's, I began to glaze over. "But," I blurted out, "what specifically are you looking for in this Plan and what do you want it to look like?" Turned out this was one of the best questions I have ever asked in my entire life. He pulled out three sample plans. Two of them were thick with pages and they looked complicated. One was about 12 pages long and looked clean and neat and not too scary.

After hemming and hawing a little, he handed me the template for the

12 pager. "You know," he said with a smile, "this is really all we need to know for a loan your size." In his world a loan of $100,000 was small potatoes, but to me it was a veritable fortune. I was so thankful for the easier template. Now, THIS was something that I could sink my teeth into.

We put that Business Plan together. Rhonda and her husband and I worked on it together. Rhonda's husband actually set up the spread sheets as I recall. We all gathered facts and numbers and he plugged them all in to a useable report. We were all so busy with our respective assignments for pulling all of this off that some of the early activities are a bit of a blur. However, much to our delight, one day we looked at each other with these big, goofy grins--it was done and ready to go!

I do have to take a moment to mention my thoughts on a Business Plan after having been through one. In my opinion, a business plan is simply a story - an educated guess at best. There are no hard numbers or history to substantiate much, if any, of this type of plan. At best it represents a logical guess which, in our case, was laced pretty heavily with optimism and wishful thinking.

In hindsight it wasn't very accurate. It wasn't very accurate at all, especially given how quickly our growth overtook our forecasts and what our expenses and staffing actually turned out to be. The numbers we actually experienced were very different than that which we anticipated. It did give us a basis, however. We tweaked that plan after the first six months and every year thereafter, until we had a pretty good guideline to use. The key to any good business is a good plan. Sometimes plans and real life don't gel at first blush! You have to keep correcting and refining as you go. Don't forget this. It will apply to all facets of your life.

VIII

So, we had the plan and we had the money. Now, we had to find our space, negotiate our lease, design it and build it out, carpet it, paint it, purchase our furniture and office equipment and purchase all of our medical equipment. Easy peasy! Not!

I thought the first part of this venture was time consuming and hard! The Business Plan was just the prep work. I equate it to repainting a room. First you are busy emptying that room, washing down the walls, scraping the old peeling paint off, filling in all the existing nail holes with spackle, sanding them smooth after the spackle dries then putting on two coats of primer – all done in anticipation of the final paint job for that room. The prep is very time consuming and must be solidly well done if the end product is to turn out beautifully. The actual painting of the color onto the walls is the fun part and, believe it or not, it is also the easiest part. It's the part that brings that room to life with each stroke of the brush. It is the part that you will see for many years to come. As fun as this phase is, better make sure that the color you have chosen is the right one or the process begins all over again.

While all that was going on, yet another phase had begun. We started researching and negotiating contractual agreements with various insurance carriers including Medicare. All the compliance and application procedures were difficult to navigate, unclear and hard to execute. Lots of questions, tenacity, blood, sweat and, yes, more tears- mostly of frustration. Many late nights, worry, nail biting, self-doubt, fervent prayers, little victories and some big victories all rolled up into a casserole of many layers and flavors, frosted with a lot of sleepless nights.

Have I scared you away yet?

I reiterate business ownership is not for the fainthearted! I say, tongue in cheek, that starting your own business is kind of like getting married or having children. It might be a good thing that we don't know what we are getting into, or we might not do it! Everything is harder, takes longer, and is more expensive than we initially think it should be.

As all this was being pulled together, yet another phase began…staffing. Our business started out with just the two of us: Rhonda, as the medical end, and me as the business end. Most of our contracts were in place except for a few stragglers that ended up taking nearly eighteen months to negotiate and execute. Our space was built, all gorgeous and ready for action. We hosted our Open House on Friday the 13th of May 2005. It was a booming smash! All of our family and friends attended. It still gives me such a warm feeling to know that people were so kind and supportive.

A day or two later we had our first non-family or friend patient! Whoo Whoo! After she had her treatment and left our office, Rhonda and I had a monumental moment! We put ONE file folder into our four-high file cabinet - one lone folder. Then we both did the happy dance around this folder and chanted as we danced, pointing our fingers and singing to the files, "grow, grow, grow!" I asked Rhonda, "Can you even *imagine* when this cabinet will be full of files?"

In time, those cabinets were bulging with files. We had to sort them every couple of months because we just couldn't cram any more in. Always a new challenge—where to store them so they are HIPAA compliant and easily accessible by staff. A good problem to have!

One thing you can count on in a business, just like in life— is the constant ongoing flux of change. You have to anticipate and manage that flux if you are to succeed and maintain some semblance of sanity!

I want to say a little about some of the most important lessons I learned about staffing. Most owners hire fast and fire slow. Most of us really don't like confrontation so we don't address personnel issues. We avoid them and hope they will improve. Crazy, huh? Hence, a borderline problem employee is tolerated for far too long and slowly poisons the morale and office atmosphere. If you let it go long enough, it permeates the entire office and the origin of the problem gets harder and harder to pinpoint. Nip those problems early on and you will save yourself a lot of headaches.

My Coach was a very important part of our growth both as a business and individually as Business Owners. As revenues, patient load and staff grew, we knew we needed to leverage the employees that were already on our payroll to accommodate our growth. Just adding bodies to chaos, without defining and clarifying roles very specifically, makes more chaos and is a great money and time waster. So, how could we leverage what we already had?

Here's a great analogy. You have a bus. Do you know exactly what the seats on your bus are? Do you know what those seats look like? Do you know the materials that they need to be made of? Do you know what each of those seats is supposed to provide? Do you know how those seats provide the things they are supposed to provide?

Once you have established these parameters, decide how many of those seats you need. Are the right people sitting in those seats? It takes a long time to plan. (Here we are on "plan" again—you beginning to understand the importance of a plan?) It takes a lot of effort to put the right person in that seat. Firing and rehiring is very costly on all levels. A good rule of thumb as to the costs associated with turnover is: Entry level employees can cost 2-3 times a year's worth of wages, depending on the specific skill set. Managers can cost 3-4 times, and Senior Managers and Executives upwards of 5 times.

Hire slow and fire fast. If you have the wrong person in that seat, take them out. If the seat is designed wrong, fix it! If you have too many seats on your bus, remove one. This analogy helped me to grasp the mechanics of a solid hiring/firing process, and an onboarding process for that matter.

IX

7 years into this enterprise, we worked out the kinks. I went from a 70 -80 hour work week to a 35 hour work week, including community service. I was making good money. I was ready to open a second location. I had grasped what the Coach was teaching me. I went from owning a job that depended on me being present or accessible 24/7, to owning a business. A business is a commercial profitable, enterprise that *runs without you. Without you* is the key.

I could now take a vacation without worries because my staff was fully knowledgeable and trained to handle the work while I was away from the office. They knew the code of conduct, the mission, vision, values and they knew what our goals were for the year. They were fully equipped and, wonderfully, were now vested in this clinic's success as never before.

I was now available to open a second location. My margins would be lovely because all of my hard costs were housed in the main clinic Increased revenue at less cost is a beautiful thing, indeed! We were now in a position to leverage our hard work. I was now in a position of CHOICE. (Thank you very much, Coach!)

We had a healthy bank account for the first time since we opened our doors. We had effectively increased our average dollar sale without compromising our patient care. Did we have to change patient care Yes, but so did everyone else. As Obama Care came into play and reimbursements for insurance, including Medicare were reduced, so was our capacity to continue treating status quo. We had to change with the times while keeping patient care to the highest standards. Challenging, but in time, with a lot of testing and measuring, we worked it out. (Again, thank you, Coach.)

We did our homework and laid our foundation. We now had a solid basis to build on. It was time to open a second location!

X

Oops! What happened? Suddenly Rhonda and I realized that we did not share the same values, life dreams or vision for our clinic's future. She had attained her goals and was quite satisfied with one clinic. I had dreams of expanding into more locations and maybe even franchising our business model.

Yikes, this is it, I thought. This is the end of the line? We were stagnant; at least that's how I felt. This is it for the rest of my life? One clinic, limited to the revenues that one clinic can generate? Yes I admit that it was a good salary; but how could I realize my legacy if I didn't have an adequate platform? This platform was limited.

What else could I do but follow my heart?

Much to Rhonda's delight, I sold my shares to her. It was a win-win. Rhonda reiterated that she had realized her dream and she was very happy with this outcome. She would attain her life's dream and I would be free to pursue my own dreams.

I could never have learned what I learned without this union. It prepared me for the next phase of my life. Rhonda says the same thing; that she would never be where she is today without our partnership. With the great advantage of two peoples' efforts, hard work, passion and contribution combined with a great coach who had much more experience than we did, look how far we had come!

Selling to Rhonda was bittersweet. It was hard to let the familiar go. Hard to let the stability go, but also really exciting and downright scary to move on to the next phase, whatever that was to be. Though exhilarating to begin anew, life was still laced with doubt, fear and what if's.

Then my story took a mind-blowing and stunningly unexpected twist. Suddenly, after a thirty year marriage, my husband made a choice that was absolutely and completely out of the realm of possibility to me. In an unbelievably surreal moment I watched him walk into the sunset with another woman.

I was astounded, blindsided, sucker punched and left totally devastated.

In the blink of an eye I was a newly divorced and single parent. These developments coupled with the sale of my business gave me the distinctive and dubious honor of tacking "unemployed" onto that sudden and unwanted description which I reluctantly carried in my new station in life.

At age fifty-two I found myself in a whole new existence stripped of everything that was familiar. Holy cow, was I frightened! I had been propelled into a horrifying and foreign realm.

For a time, after these new and unwelcomed upheavals, I was stuck - stuck behind a line that separated the old from the new, the past from the future. From what *was* to what *could be*. I stood there a long time afraid and rooted in the past. After some serious soul searching, a faith journey and some therapy, one day I just decided to take a deep breath, brace myself for what might come, and cross that line.

It's said that the journey of 1,000 miles begins with the first step.

So I took that leap of faith, and instantly knew it was the right thing to do. I was on my way to my new beginning. This time, though, I was a woman with a little more wisdom, a little more experience, a little more strength, a little more confidence and something that I did not have before—faith. I am following my heart and I am finding my way.

Life is like a roller coaster. It has surprising twists and hair pin curves that can leave us breathless. Much to my surprise, I was invited by my former coach to join his firm. I learned very quickly that I was joining a business that was still in its fledgling stages. So once again, I would have a business to build. It was kind of like having another child. I asked myself, could I do it again? Would I love this one as much as the others? Would I have the energy to complete the task? Could I bring this entity into a new life? Would it be a good life?

These days, I find myself on the ground floor of building both another business and a whole new life. It is a place that I once considered completely unimaginable, a terrifying place that I would never have ventured into willingly. Yet here I am just the same. Though nothing is familiar and the landscape looks both terrifying and hugely challenging on every level, there is a part of me that relishes every moment of it.

God has totally blessed me. I am part of a company that I absolutely love. Every day at our office does not feel like work because I enjoy it so much. How many people get to do the thing they love most for a living? What could be more fulfilling than helping other business owners reach their dreams?

Not every day is easy—not by a long shot. There are still times when I doubt. There are still times when I despair. There are still times, during dark and bleak nights, that I find myself sobbing out my troubles. There are still times when I wonder just what is to become of me.

Yes, here I am, still alive and able to work and breathe and walk and live; still able to dream, still able to build a future. That platform is still within reach.

Oh, and I am happy to say that God has blessed me once again. He brought a very special man into my life. And now, once again, I find myself standing behind a line. But this time I am not alone. Together, hand in hand, we take yet another leap of faith as we step over that line to begin a new life. I pray it will be a wild but good ride!

The end? Perhaps this is really just another beginning...

May you enjoy many wonderful beginnings throughout your life and I pray yours will be a wild but good ride too!

Dedication

This is dedicated to my children: Kyla, Jenice, Grant, Jacob and Marta for their ongoing strength and support during both my darkest and my brightest moments; my Mother and my Father, John and Betty Lou for their endless patience and love; my sister, Wendy, and my brother, Kurt, for being there at any hour; my adopted bros Kevin and Robert who honor me by calling me "sis"; my big family of in-laws whom I will love forever, especially Karen who saved my life, Julie who held me even when she was across "the pond", and Jack the rock of the family; Lettie, MB and my Cennical sisters for showing me the path and continuing to pick me up when I stumble; my friends Kim, Tricia, Sharon, and the Lisa's three, and all those too numerous to mention - you know who you are – without you I could not have healed – bless you for your endless patience; and Dave, my business partner and my very best friend in this whole wide world—my Dave who never has and never will give up on me. Bless you Dave and your wonder-ful family who have embraced me with open hearts and open arms; and to all people whose lives are suddenly shattered. There IS light at the end of that long, dark and seemingly endless tunnel. Faith, trust, hope, and above all God's love, will see you through.

Thank you, Lord for all my blessings - those that hurt and taught me and those that pleased and enlightened me - and for this journey— this wild ride, this good ride, this crazy ride we call life!

About Bonnie

Bonnie is now partner and VP of Business Development at Peak Performance/ActionCOACH.

Bonnie and her team of Business Coaches enrich lives both at work and at home by providing solutions to the problems that keep business owners up at night worrying. Enjoy more sleep filled nights, more time off, more vacations and more worry-free days. Learn how to apply our proven methodologies to improve every aspect of your business so you too can enjoy more money, more time and more peace of mind. You CAN live your dreams!

Bonnie can be contacted via email at: authorbonnierichtman@gmail. com

Invitations for Public Speaking engagements are welcomed!

CPSIA information can be obtained
at www.ICGtesting.com
Printed in the USA
FFOW01n0204030316
21992FF